LAMP LIGHT

Living

TABLE OF
Contents

CURRICULUM
Cycles

As a wife and mom of four, I have learned to live my life by saying, "If the Lord wills." I have learned that the plans in my heart aren't always established by God, and that it is better to start with humility than confidence when it comes to taking on projects.

That being said, it has been my hope since the Lord called me to the project of "That It May Go Well" to make it a multi-cycle curriculum. I have had questions about how each guide is to be used. I thought it would be helpful to share some of that vision here with the disclaimer that this will happen if the Lord wills!

That It May Go Well
VISION

- Three cycles designed to rotate through grades K-5, each cycle is used twice over the course of the elementary school years.
- Consumable student guides, reusable teacher guides.
- Preschool that can be used along with any of the cycles (or standalone).
- Different topics covered each year that make for well-rounded learning.
- Always free of charge to download.
- Printed copies for a very reasonable price.
- The option to print wherever you choose. (And to possibly get reimbursed for those expenses, if you are enrolled in a charter school. You are, after all, not paying for any "religious" material or books that mention God but simply printing costs!)
- What comes after grade 5? Only the Lord knows! This project is currently growing with our family. With the help and strength of the Lord, my hope is to be able to make the upcoming year that our children will need each year and to be able to offer those to you.
- <u>What can you do?</u> PRAY! I sincerely appreciate your prayers for my family and I as we work on this project. Beyond that, please share with your friends, neighbors, church, and social media pages. It is a sweet blessing to get this into the hands of believers around the world!

PLEASE *Note*

That It May Go Well is designed for use with both the teacher guide and student workbook. Without the teacher guide, it is not truly an all in one curriculum as much of the information is found within the teacher guide.

You will find that the teacher guide is not a traditional teacher's guide. It is where the bulk of the Biblical information, memory verses, and Bible reading recommendations are located.

WELCOME!

Welcome to a new school year! This book is written primarily to students, although for second-grade students you should plan to read most of their assignments to them and help them review their daily checklist. You may wish to reduce some assignments for second-grade students.

UNIT
One

SPELLING LISTS

Your student's spelling words will come from words you identify that they spell incorrectly in their writing. Because of this, spelling does not start until week 2. As your student writes for assignments (or any other writing), please write the words they spell incorrectly here. At the end of the week, there will be a spelling quiz. If your student continues to struggle with a word, add it to the following week's list.

Week 2	Week 3	Week 4

WEEK 1, DAY 1

DAILY TASKS

☐ Bible verse penmanship practice

☐ Practice your spelling words (does not begin until week 2)

☐ Individual reading time for 15-20 minutes

☐ Complete worksheets in your workbook

☐ Work on your unit art project or handicraft

BIBLE JOURNALING

Please write one sentence about something you learned that was meaningful to you from our Bible time today.

_____

_____

_____

_____

_____

_____

_____

_____

_____

_____

Please draw a picture of something I read about from the Bible.

Please practice writing this part of our memory verse.

In the beginning God created the heavens
and the earth.
Genesis 1:1

Sight word review: Please read these to me. Please practice any words you struggle with until you are confident reading them.

always	cold	green
around	does	its
because	don't	made
been	fast	many
before	first	off
best	five	or
both	found	pull
buy	gave	read
call	goes	write

Table of Contents

Turn to the front of your Bible. Here you can find the table of contents. Most books have a table of contents. The table of contents tells you the page number where you can find specific chapters. In the Bible, the table of contents tells the page number where you can find each book of the Bible.

What page is Genesis on? _____

What page is John on? _____

BIBLE VERSE

>>>>>>>>>>   <<<<<<<<<<

With the help of your parents, please choose a Bible verse from one of the chapters we read this week to verse map.

*Note to parents: Please review the grammar focus, and try to assist your child in choosing a passage that will contain multiple opportunities to practice this principle.

- Work with your parent to study this verse. Talk about what it means.

- Look up any words you do not understand.

Grammar Focus:

A noun is a person, place, or thing. Proper nouns are specific persons, places, or things, and should have their first letter capitalized.

Examples:

Noun: boy | Proper noun: Adam

Noun: garden | Proper noun: Eden

Please circle all nouns in the verse you choose to write. Star any proper nouns.

_____

_____

_____

_____

_____

_____

_____

CREATION
SCAVENGER HUNT

 1 A light stick and a dark stick (best to have these be at least as thick as your thumb and about 18 inches long)

 2 A cloud that looks like a letter of the alphabet

 3 12-20 flat rocks (these will be used for making story rocks) + 3 plants that produce seeds (dry and save for a project)

 4 A picture of you in the sunshine

 5 Spot a bird. What kind of bird did you see?

_____

 6 Spot an animal. How did it react to you? What did God say about people and animals?

 7 Take a moment to rest. Look around and name 7 things you are thankful that God created. Remember God called His creation good!

Bonus:

DAILY TASKS

☐ Bible verse penmanship practice

☐ Practice your spelling words (does not begin until week 2)

☐ Individual reading time for 15-20 minutes

☐ Complete worksheets in your workbook

☐ History/Geography

MY DAY

Please fill in this information about your day.

DATE: _____ / ___ / _____

WEATHER

TIME: _____

8

Please practice writing this part of our memory verse.

In the beginning God created the heavens
and the earth.
Genesis 1:1

Writing is one of the most important skills you will learn. We have to learn to write good sentences in order to write good stories and papers. Writing helps you to express yourself, make requests, and tell stories. You will use writing skills almost every day throughout your life.

Here is a review of some main parts of a well-written sentence:

- [ ] Begins with a capital letter
- [ ] Noun- a person, place, or thing
- [ ] Verb- an action word or state of being
- [ ] Punctuation- all sentences end with punctuation

Examples: period .   question mark ?   exclamation point !

Please use this checklist to write two sentences about what we have learned about God creating the heavens and the earth. Include details about the first people God created.

_____

_____

_____

_____

_____

_____

_____

 # CONTINENTS

Please fill in the correct answer from the word bank.

continents	land mass	7 days
oceans	day 3	dry land

1. A continent is a _____

2. There are 7_____ on earth.

3. There are 4 _____on earth.

4. It took God _____to create the heavens and the earth.

5. What day did God create dry land?_____

Which continent do you

live on?

_____

_____

DAILY TASKS

☐ Bible verse penmanship practice

☐ Practice your spelling words (does not begin until week 2)

☐ Individual reading time for 15-20 minutes

☐ Complete worksheets in your workbook

☐ Science

JOURNALING MY WEEK

Please write 1-2 sentences about your week. You may choose to tell something you have learned, done, or experienced.

_____

_____

_____

_____

_____

_____

_____

_____

Please practice writing this part of our memory verse.

In the beginning God created the heavens and the earth.
Gensis 1:1

Today we read about Jesus calling some of his disciples. I would like you to imagine what it would have been like to be called to follow Jesus. Please write a short story about what this would have been like. Don't forget to check your sentences for capital letters, correct punctuation, and complete thoughts. Use extra paper if needed.

LET THERE BE LIGHT
SCIENCE WORKSHEET

1. What day did God create light?

_____

_____

2. What is created when light shines around an object?

_____

_____

3. What does light generate?

_____

_____

Please draw a picture of your observations from our activity.

OBSERVATIONS

DAILY TASKS

☐ Bible verse penmanship practice *Choose a sheet from the end of the book on day 4 of each week for writing your memory verse

☐ Spelling test (not until week 2)

☐ Individual reading time for 15-20 minutes

☐ Complete worksheets in your workbook

☐ Check your work for the week, review anything that felt challenging

FACT OF THE WEEK

Please read this information. It is fun to learn new things!

VOLCANOES

A volcano is a mountain or hill that has a vent, or opening, through which hot magma, gases, and other materials erupt from deep inside the Earth. When a volcano erupts, it can release lava, ash, steam, and rocks into the air or onto the surrounding land.

15

Read the following paragraph and find any errors. Circle letters that should be capitalized.

Remember- These should always be capitalized:
The word "I"
The first letter of a sentence
Proper nouns (names of specific people, places, or things)
Look for missing punctuation and add where needed.

jesus was in the beginning when God created the heavens and the earth. what would it have been like to be there   I am so thankful that God created all of the beautiful trees, fruit, fish, and animals. adam and eve were the first people that God created. it makes me sad that sin entered the world. i am so thankful that Jesus died for my sins

Please draw a line from the word to the definition.

Fiction   Books that are a true story or factual.

Non-Fiction   Books that are not based on true events.

DAILY TASKS

☐ Bible verse penmanship practice

☐ Practice your spelling words

☐ Individual reading time for 15-20 minutes

☐ Complete worksheets in your workbook

☐ Work on your unit art project or handicraft

BIBLE JOURNALING

Please write one sentence about something you learned that was meaningful to you from our Bible time today.

_____

_____

_____

_____

_____

_____

_____

_____

Please practice writing this part of our memory verse.

Trust in the Lord with all your heart and lean
not on your own understanding.
Proverbs 3:5

Please read these to me. Mark any words that your student struggles with. Please practice any words your child struggles with until they are confident reading them. Review last week's list if needed.

about	eight	if
better	fall	keep
bring	far	kind
carry	full	laugh
clean	got	light
cut	grow	long
done	hold	much
draw	hot	myself
drink	hurt	never

Antonyms-
are words that mean the opposite. For example "hot" and "cold" or "up" and "down." Please write the opposite of the following words.

in _____

on _____

high _____

sweet _____

happy _____

Draw the opposite.

BIBLE VERSE
MAPPING

With the help of your parents, please choose a Bible verse from one of the chapters we read this week to verse map.

*Note to parents: Please review the grammar focus. Try to assist your child in choosing a passage that will contain multiple opportunities to practice this principle.

- Work with your parent to study this verse. Talk about what it means.

- Look up any words you do not understand.

Grammar Focus:

A noun is a person, place, or thing. Proper nouns are specific persons, places, or things and should have their first letter capitalized.

Examples:

Noun: boy | Proper noun: Adam

Noun: garden | Proper noun: Eden

Please circle all nouns in the verse you choose to write. Star any proper nouns.

_____

_____

_____

_____

_____

_____

_____

DAILY TASKS

☐ Bible verse penmanship practice

☐ Practice your spelling words

☐ Individual reading time for 15-20 minutes

☐ Complete worksheets in your workbook

☐ History/Geography

MY DAY

Please fill in this information about your day.

DATE: _____ / _____ / _____

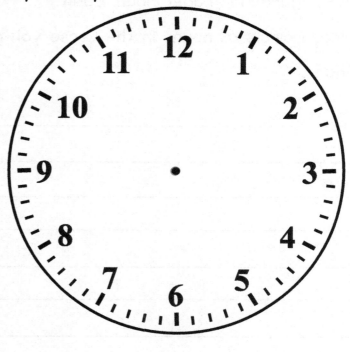

WEATHER

TIME: _____

Please draw a picture of something I read about from the Bible.

Please practice writing this part of our memory verse.

Trust in the Lord with all your heart and lean
not on your own understanding.
Proverbs 3:5

Today we are going to learn about paragraphs. Paragraphs are multiple sentences that are about the same idea. Paragraphs are made up of three parts: a topic sentence, supporting sentences, and a closing sentence. In the topic sentence you will introduce your theme or topic, in the supporting sentences you will give details, and in the closing sentence you will restate the focus of the paragraph. You can imagine it like a sandwich. Look at this diagram.

Topic sentence /Bread ————————————

Supporting sentences/Filling ————

Closing sentence/Bread —————

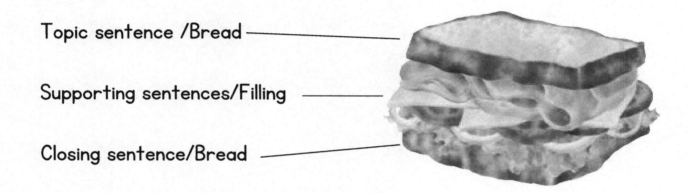

We can use multiple paragraphs together to write a paper, a letter, or a report. When we write, there are five questions we need to answer. These help the reader to understand the full idea we wish to convey. These are the "5 Ws." When we write multiple paragraphs to form a paper, we indent each paragraph.

Who

What

When

Where

Why

When we talk about including the five 5 W's in writing, remember these. Let's practice using these now.

CONTINENT STUDY
ANTARCTICA

Work with your parent to get these answers from books or the internet.

1. Where is this continent located? What hemisphere(s) is it in?
_____
_____

2. What is the climate?
_____
_____

3. What oceans are near this continent?
_____
_____

4. How many countries are on this continent?
_____
_____

5. What is the population?
_____
_____

6. How large is this continent?
_____
_____

7. What are the top natural resources?
_____
_____

8. What are the main religions?
_____
_____

DAILY TASKS

☐ Bible verse penmanship practice

☐ Practice your spelling words

☐ Individual reading time for 15-20 minutes

☐ Complete worksheets in your workbook

☐ Science 💡

BOOK SUMMARY

Please write a short summary of a book you have been reading for your individual reading time.

TITLE: _____

AUTHOR: _____

_____
_____
_____
_____
_____

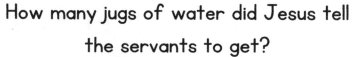
How many jugs of water did Jesus tell the servants to get?

Jesus changed water to

_____

Please practice writing this part of our memory verse.

Trust in the Lord with all your heart and lean
not on your own understanding.
Proverbs 3:5

_____

_____

_____

_____

_____

SPELLING
PRACTICE

Please write each of your spelling words two times.

_____   _____

_____   _____

_____   _____

_____   _____

_____   _____

_____   _____

_____   _____

_____   _____

Please write two sentences using at least three of your spelling words.

_____

_____

_____

_____

_____

RAINBOWS OF LIGHT
SCIENCE WORKSHEET

1. Why did God create the rainbow? What does the rainbow show us? _____

_____

2. Name some types of light that cannot be seen. _____

_____

3. When light shines through water it creates a _____:

_____

Please draw a picture of your observations from our activity.

OBSERVATIONS

DAILY TASKS

☐ Bible verse penmanship practice

☐ Spelling test

☐ Individual reading time for 15-20 minutes

☐ Complete worksheets in your workbook

☐ Check your work for the week, review anything that felt challenging

FACT OF THE WEEK

Please read this information. It is fun to learn new things!

ECOSYSTEMS

An ecosystem is a community of living things interacting together in their physical environment.

Ecosystems can be aquatic (in or near water) or terrestrial (on land). In the coming weeks you will have facts about various ecosystems.

- Write the definitions of the colored/underlined words by looking them up in a dictionary or online. Write them next to the coordinating star. Include the part of speech.
- Circle the <u>nouns</u> in this passage.

"Noah was a <u>righteous</u> man, blameless among the people of his time, and he walked <u>faithfully</u> with God." Genesis 6:9

★ _____
_____
_____
_____

★ _____
_____
_____
_____

HISTORICAL
PERSON OF INTEREST

Please choose a person you have learned about to answer these questions and write a report. You may need your parent to help you locate these facts using the internet or the book you have been reading. On the back, please write one paragraph about this person.

1. Who are you learning about?

_____

_____

2. What did they do?

_____

_____

3. When did they live?

_____

_____

4. Where did they live?

_____

_____

5. Why would someone be interested in learning about this person?

_____

_____

_____

_____

_____

_____

Write one paragraph about the person you have chosen. Be sure to include their name, why they are interesting, where they lived, and when they lived there. Imagine you are writing to someone who knows nothing about the person you are writing about.

<u>Paragraph Check List</u>

☐ Topic sentence

☐ Supporting sentences

☐ Closing sentence

☐ The 5 Ws

_____

_____

_____

_____

_____

_____

_____

_____

_____

_____

_____

_____

_____

_____

_____

_____

DAILY TASKS

☐ Bible verse penmanship practice

☐ Practice your spelling words

☐ Individual reading time for 15-20 minutes

☐ Complete worksheets in your workbook

☐ Work on your unit art project or handicraft

BIBLE JOURNALING

Please write one sentence about something you learned that was meaningful to you from our Bible time today.

_____

_____

_____

_____

_____

_____

_____

_____

Please draw a picture of something I read about from the Bible.

Please practice writing this part of our memory verse.

And the scripture was fulfilled that says,
"Abraham believed God, and it was credited
to him as righteousness," and he was called
God's friend.
James 2:23

<u>Homophones</u> are words that sound the same but are spelled differently and have different meanings. Today we will practice <u>to, too, and two.</u>

To: a preposition that shows motion

Too: an adverb that is used to describe something "in addition" or a way to say "also" or "as well"

Two: the written form of the number 2

Write a sentence using the word <u>to.</u>

_____

_____

_____

Write a sentence using the word <u>too.</u>

_____

_____

_____

Write a sentence using the word <u>two.</u>

_____

_____

_____

<u>Abbreviations</u> are letters we use to shorten and represent commonly used words. Today we will practice <u>mister to Mr., missus to Mrs., miss to Ms., and doctor to Dr.</u> Please write the abbreviation for each of these words.

Mister: _____

Missus: _____

Miss: _____

Doctor: _____

BIBLE VERSE

MAPPING

With the help of your parents, please choose a Bible verse from one of the chapters we read this week to verse map.

*Note to parents: Please review the grammar focus. Try to assist your child in choosing a passage that will contain multiple opportunities to practice this principle.

- Work with your parent to study this verse. Talk about what it means.

- Look up any words you do not understand.

Grammar Focus:

A verb is a word that shows action or state of being. Today we are going to work on words that show action. Examples: run, sit, hop, hopping, running, jumping, talking, jumped, ate, walked

- Please underline all words that show action.
- Please circle all nouns in the verse you choose to write.
- Please star any proper nouns.

_____

_____

_____

_____

_____

_____

_____

DAILY TASKS

☐ Bible verse penmanship practice

☐ Practice your spelling words

☐ Individual reading time for 15-20 minutes

☐ Complete worksheets in your workbook

☐ History/Geography

MY DAY

Please fill in this information about your day.

DATE: ___ / ___ / ___

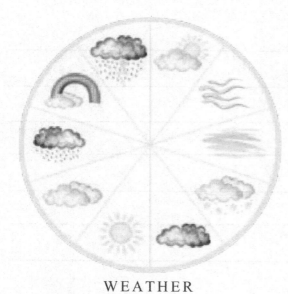

WEATHER

TIME: _____

Please practice writing this part of our memory verse.

And the scripture was fulfilled that says, "Abraham believed God, and it was credited to him as righteousness," and he was called God's friend.
James 2:23

CONTINENT STUDY
ANTARCTICA

Today you are going to take the information you learned last week and make it into a poster report. Please include a picture of the continent, details about the population, size, and climate. Share your report with your family or friends and tell them about the continent you studied.

Population:

Size:

Climate:

ANTARCTICA

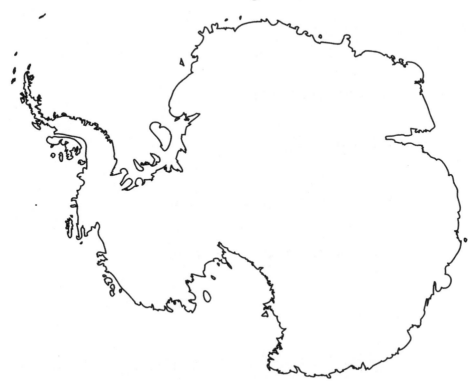

- Please label the 3 largest cities, use a red dot to mark.
- Draw in any major rivers or lakes with blue colored pencil
- If the <u>equator</u> crosses this continent please draw a black line to show where.
- Please label the oceans around this continent.

Name of this continent:

_____

_____

What is the primary reason people live on Antarctica? Why aren't there permanent residents there?

Why aren't there any countries on Antarctica?

_____

_____

_____

_____

DAILY TASKS

☐ Bible verse penmanship practice

☐ Practice your spelling words

☐ Individual reading time for 15-20 minutes

☐ Complete worksheets in your workbook

☐ Science 💡

JOURNALING MY WEEK

Please write 1-2 sentences about your week. You may choose to tell something you have learned, done, or experienced.

_____

_____

_____

_____

_____

_____

_____

_____

_____

Please draw a picture of something I read about from the Bible.

Please practice writing this part of our memory verse.

And the scripture was fulfilled that says,
"Abraham believed God, and it was credited
to him as righteousness," and he was called
God's friend.
James 2:23

SPELLING
PRACTICE

Please write each of your spelling words two times.

_____   _____

_____   _____

_____   _____

_____   _____

_____   _____

_____   _____

_____   _____

WRITE A LETTER

*Parents: Help your child write a properly formatted letter including a greeting, body, closing, and signature. (If you struggle to remember this, look up "personal letter format." Don't forget to add any misspelled words to your child's spelling list. Explain placement of the address, return address, and stamp. Tell your child the price of a stamp.

Please write a letter of encouragement to someone. Have your parent edit your letter. Correct any mistakes in spelling or grammar.

Address the envelope for your letter and put your return address with the help of your parent. Each time you send a letter, you will get more confident in this. Use good penmanship so the post office can easily read what you wrote.

HOW LIGHT IS USED
SCIENCE WORKSHEET

1. How do plants eat? What is this called?

_____

_____

2. What do plants breathe out during the day?

How does this help the air? _____

_____

3. Plants need light to produce _____ .

Please draw a picture of your observations from our activity.

OBSERVATIONS

DAILY TASKS

☐ Bible verse penmanship practice

☐ Spelling test

☐ Individual reading time for 15-20 minutes

☐ Complete worksheets in your workbook

☐ Check your work for the week, review anything that felt challenging

FACT OF THE WEEK

Please read this information. It is fun to learn new things!

ECOSYSTEMS   Savannah

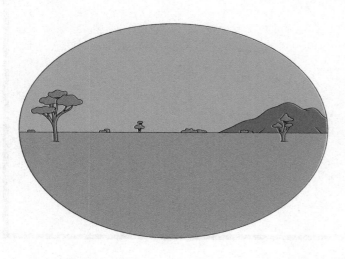

A grassland environment with scattered trees allowing light to reach the ground.

BIBLE VERSE

MAPPING

- Write the definitions of the colored/underlined words by looking them up in a dictionary or online. Write them next to the coordinating star. Include the part of speech.

- Circle the <u>nouns</u> in this passage.

- Underline the <u>verbs</u> in this passage

Then God said to Abraham, "As for you, you must keep my <u>covenant</u>, you and your <u>descendants</u> after you for the generations to come." Genesis 17:9

★ _____
_____
_____
_____

★ _____
_____
_____
_____

STORIES FROM SCRIPTURE
WRITING PROJECT

Please choose one of the stories we have read from the Bible this week to write about. Imagine you are telling the story to someone who has never heard it. Tell them why you like this story and what it means to you. Answer the 5 W questions to help you write. Use additional notebook paper if needed.

Who? _____

What? _____

When? _____

Where? _____

Why? _____

_____

_____

_____

_____

_____

_____

_____

_____

_____

DAILY TASKS

☐ Bible verse penmanship practice

☐ Practice your spelling words

☐ Individual reading time for 15-20 minutes

☐ Complete worksheets in your workbook

☐ Work on your unit art project or handicraft

BIBLE JOURNALING

Please write one sentence about something you learned that was meaningful to you from our Bible time today.

_____

_____

_____

_____

_____

_____

_____

_____

_____

Please draw a picture of something I read about from the Bible.

Please practice writing this part of our memory verse.

Your descendants will be like the dust of the
earth, and you will spread out to the west
and to the east, to the north and to the
south. All peoples on earth will be blessed
through you and your offspring.
Genesis 28:14

Punctuation- You are familiar with punctuation. Periods, exclamation points, and question marks are all punctuation. There are other types of punctuation too, such as commas, quotations, and apostrophes. We are going to practice commas today. Commas show a pause in a sentence. Today we are going to practice lists and dates.

List Example: Each day I read my Bible, pray, and worship God.
Please write a sentence with a list separated by commas.

_____

_____

_____

_____

Date Example: America became a country July 4, 1776.
Dates are also written in numerical format. This is often how they are written when dating a document. Example: 07/04/1776
Please write today's date in both a sentence and in numerical format.

_____

_____

_____

_____

Today's date: _____ / _____ / _____

BIBLE VERSE
MAPPING

With the help of your parents, please choose a Bible verse from one of the chapters we read this week to verse map.

*Note to parents: Please review the grammar focus. Try to assist your child in choosing a passage that will contain multiple opportunities to practice this principle.

- Work with your parent to study this verse. Talk about what it means.

- Look up any words you do not understand.

Grammar Focus:

Pronouns are words that take the place of a noun in a sentence. Please ask your parent to show you the list of pronouns.

Here is an example: Jacob sent gifts. He sent gifts.

The word "he" replaces Jacob.

- Box any pronouns

- Please underline all words that show action.

- Please circle all nouns.

- Please star any proper nouns.

_____

_____

_____

_____

_____

_____

_____

DAILY TASKS

☐ Bible verse penmanship practice

☐ Practice your spelling words

☐ Individual reading time for 15-20 minutes

☐ Complete worksheets in your workbook

☐ History/Geography 🕐 🌐

MY DAY

Please fill in this information about your day.

DATE: _____ / _____ / _____

WEATHER

TIME: _____

Please practice writing this part of our memory verse.

Your descendants will be like the dust of the
earth, and you will spread out to the west
and to the east, to the north and to the
south. All peoples on earth will be blessed
through you and your offspring.
Genesis 28:14

 # MAPS

Please label the compass.

_____

_____

_____   _____

_____   _____

_____

_____

Use a map to find the answer to the following questions.

Your current location: _____

Closest river: _____

Closest lake: _____

How many miles to the nearest airport?_____

How many miles to the nearest store? _____

DAILY TASKS

☐ Bible verse penmanship practice

☐ Practice your spelling words

☐ Individual reading time for 15-20 minutes

☐ Complete worksheets in your workbook

☐ Science

BOOK SUMMARY

Please write a short summary of a book you have been reading for your individual reading time.

TITLE: _____

AUTHOR: _____

_____

_____

_____

_____

_____

Please draw a picture of something I read about from the Bible.

Please practice writing this part of our memory verse.

Your descendants will be like the dust of the earth, and you will spread out to the west and to the east, to the north and to the south. All peoples on earth will be blessed through you and your offspring.
Genesis 28:14

SPELLING
PRACTICE

Please write each of your spelling words two times.

_____   _____

_____   _____

_____   _____

_____   _____

_____   _____

_____   _____

_____   _____

Please write two sentences using at least three of your spelling words.

_____

_____

_____

_____

_____

_____

A LIGHT ON A STAND
SCIENCE ACTIVITY

Please write your observations from each of these phases of our activity. Did it give more or less light? How was the light different?

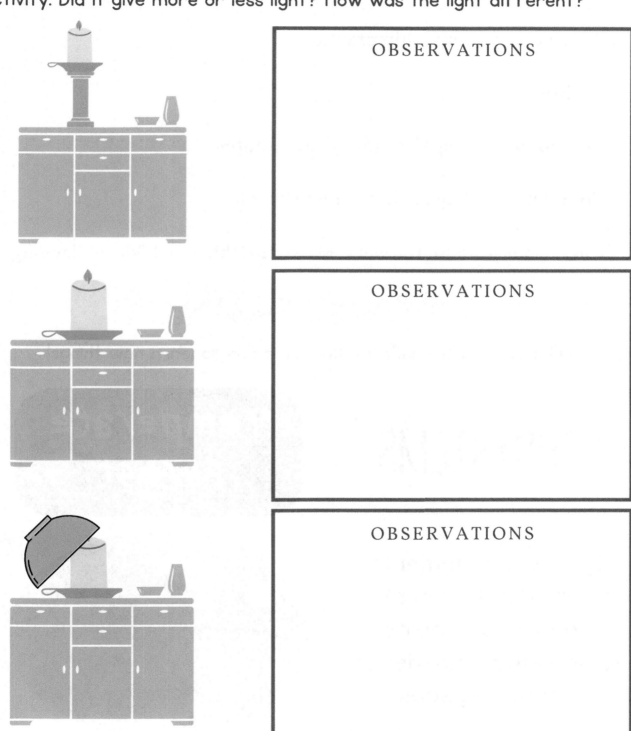

OBSERVATIONS

OBSERVATIONS

OBSERVATIONS

DAILY TASKS

☐ Bible verse penmanship practice

☐ Spelling test

☐ Individual reading time for 15-20 minutes

☐ Complete worksheets in your workbook

☐ Check your work for the week, review anything that felt challenging

FACT OF THE WEEK

Please read this information. It is fun to learn new things!

ECOSYSTEMS

Temperate Forest

Forest environments located between the tropical and polar regions that experience distinct seasons.

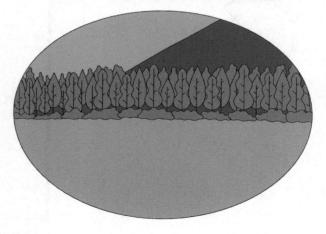

BIBLE VERSE

MAPPING

- Write the definitions of the colored/underlined words by looking them up in a dictionary or online. Write them next to the coordinating star. Include the part of speech.
- Circle the <u>nouns</u> in this passage.
- Underline the <u>verbs</u> in this passage.
- Box the <u>pronouns</u> in this passage.

"What then shall we say? Is God unjust? Not at all! For he says to Moses, 'I will have **mercy** on whom I have mercy, and I will have compassion on whom I have compassion.'

It does not, therefore, depend on human desire or <u>effort</u>, but on God's mercy."

Romans 9:14-16

★ _____

_____

_____

_____

HISTORICAL
PERSON OF INTEREST

Please choose a person you have learned about to answer these questions and write a report. You may need your parent to help you locate these facts using the internet or the book you have been reading. On the back, please write one paragraph about this person.

1. Who are you learning about?

_____

_____

2. What did they do?

_____

_____

3. When did they live?

_____

_____

4. Where did they live?

_____

_____

5. Why would someone be interested in learning about this person?

_____

_____

_____

_____

_____

_____

Write one paragraph about the person you have chosen. Be sure to include their name, why they are interesting, where they lived, and when they lived there. Imagine you are writing to someone who knows nothing about the person you are writing about.

Paragraph Check List

☐ Topic sentence

☐ Supporting sentences

☐ Closing sentence

☐ The 5 Ws

_____

_____

_____

_____

_____

_____

_____

_____

_____

_____

_____

_____

_____

_____

_____

CREATE YOUR OWN MINI UNIT STUDY

This week you will create a mini-unit study on something you wish to study. Work with your parent to come up with ideas and a plan.

Topic of Study: _____

List of ways to learn about this topic:

_____
_____
_____
_____
_____
_____

Scriptures that apply:

_____
_____
_____
_____

Field trip or activity ideas:

_____
_____
_____
_____

CREATE YOUR OWN MINI UNIT STUDY

Draw a picture of your topic of choice:

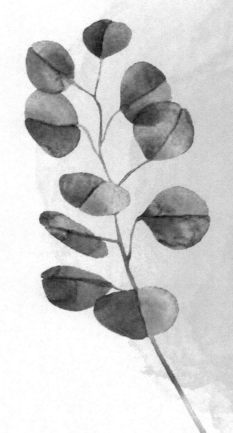

UNIT
two

UNIT
two

SPELLING LISTS

Your student's spelling words will come from words you identify that they spell incorrectly in their writing. As your student writes for assignments (or any other writing) please write the words they spell incorrectly here. At the end of the week there will be a spelling quiz. If your student continues to struggle with a word add it to the following week's list.

Week 1	Week 2	Week 3	Week 4

DAILY TASKS

☐ Bible verse penmanship practice

☐ Practice your spelling words

☐ Individual reading time for 15-20 minutes

☐ Complete worksheets in your workbook

☐ Work on your unit art project or handicraft

BIBLE JOURNALING

Please write one sentence about something you learned that was meaningful to you from our Bible time today.

_____

_____

_____

_____

_____

_____

_____

_____

_____

Please draw a picture of something I read about from the Bible.

Please practice writing this part of our memory verse.

You intended to harm me, but God intended it for good to accomplish what is now being done, the saving of many lives.

Genesis 50:20

Homophones are words that sound the same but are spelled differently and have different meanings. Today we will practice their and there.

Their: Shows belonging to a person/people. Example: This is their yard.

There: A place or location. Example: We will go there tomorrow.

Write a sentence using the word their.

_____

_____

_____

Write a sentence using the word there.

_____

_____

_____

Abbreviations are letters we use to shorten and represent commonly used words. Today we will practice the days of the week.

Sunday: Sun.

Monday: Mon.

Tuesday: Tue.

Wednesday: Wed.

Thursday: Thurs.

Friday: Fri.

Saturday: Sat.

On a separate sheet of paper please write the days of the week and the abbreviation for each.

DAILY TASKS

☐ Bible verse penmanship practice

☐ Practice your spelling words

☐ Individual reading time for 15-20 minutes

☐ Complete worksheets in your workbook

☐ History/Geography

MY DAY

Please fill in this information about your day.

DATE: _____ / _____ / _____

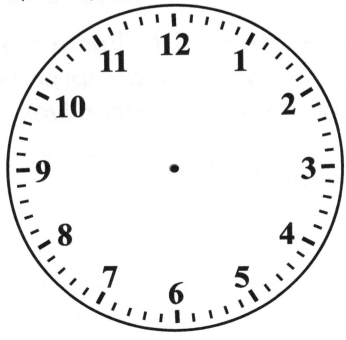

WEATHER

TIME: _____

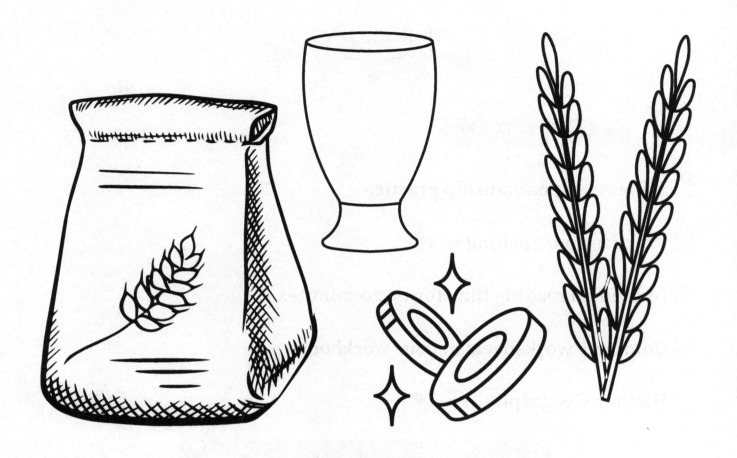

Please practice writing this part of our memory verse.

<u>You intended to harm me, but God intended it
for good to accomplish what is now being done,
the saving of many lives.</u>

<u>Genesis 50:20</u>

BIBLE VERSE
MAPPING

With the help of your parents please choose a Bible verse from one of the chapters we read this week to verse map.

*Note to parents: Please review the grammar focus, and try to assist your child in choosing a passage that will contain multiple opportunities to practice this principle.

- Work with your parent to study this verse. Talk about what it means.

- Look up any words you do not understand.

Grammar Focus:

An adjective is a word that describes a noun.

Example: "With long life I will satisfy him and show him my salvation."

Psalm 91:16

Nouns: life, salvation

Adjective: long, my

Please circle all nouns in the verse you choose to write. Underline the adjectives.

_____

_____

_____

_____

_____

_____

_____

_____

CONTINENT STUDY
AFRICA

Work with your parent to get these answers from books or the internet.

1. Where is this continent located? What hemisphere(s) is it in?

_____

_____

2. What is the climate?

_____

_____

3. What oceans are near this continent?

_____

_____

4. How many countries are on this continent?

_____

_____

5. What is the population?

_____

_____

6. How large is this continent?

_____

_____

7. What are the top natural resources?

_____

_____

8. What are the main religions?

_____

_____

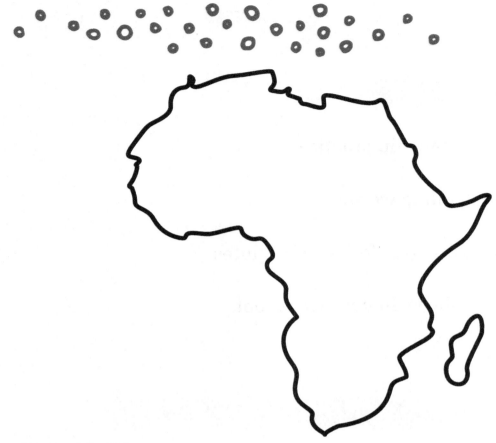

- Please label the 3 largest cities, use a red dot to mark.
- Draw in any major rivers or lakes with blue colored pencil
- If the equator crosses this continent please draw a black line to show where.
- Please label the oceans around this continent.

Name of this continent:

_____

_____

We will study one country from this continent. Please choose which country you would like to study and find resources to learn more about this country.

Country:

_____

_____

DAILY TASKS

☐ Bible verse penmanship practice

☐ Practice your spelling words

☐ Individual reading time for 15-20 minutes

☐ Complete worksheets in your workbook

☐ Science 💡

JOURNALING MY WEEK

Please write 1-2 sentences about your week. You may choose to tell something you have learned, done, or experienced.

_____

_____

_____

_____

_____

_____

_____

_____

Please practice writing this part of our memory verse.

You intended to harm me, but God intended it
for good to accomplish what is now being done,
the saving of many lives.

Genesis 50:20

H2o
SCIENCE WORKSHEET

1. What is water?

_____

_____

2. What percent of the earth is covered by water?

_____

_____

3. What are the two kinds of water found on earth? Circle which kind we drink.

_____

_____

Which state of water is best represented by each picture?

_____

_____

_____

SPELLING
PRACTICE

Please write each of your spelling words two times.

_____   _____

_____   _____

_____   _____

_____   _____

_____   _____

_____   _____

_____   _____

Please write two sentences using at least three of your spelling words.

_____

_____

_____

_____

_____

_____

DAILY TASKS

☐ Bible verse penmanship practice

☐ Spelling test

☐ Individual reading time for 15-20 minutes

☐ Complete worksheets in your workbook

☐ Check your work for the week, review anything that felt challenging

FACT OF THE WEEK

Please read this information. It is fun to learn new things!

ECOSYSTEMS   Desert

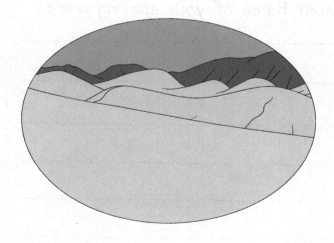

Dry environments with
sparse vegetation,
high temperatures and
low rainfall.

STORIES FROM SCRIPTURE
WRITING PROJECT

Please choose one of the stories we have read from the Bible this week to write about. Imagine you are telling the story to someone who has never heard it. Tell them why you like this story and what it means to you. Answer the 5 W questions to help you write at least one paragraph. Use notebook paper to write, or type your paper on the computer. When you are finished writing, edit your work. Check for complete sentences, proper capitalization, and punctuation. Have your parent offer suggestions for ways to improve your writing. Be sure they edit for spelling. Add any words that are incorrect to next week's spelling list.

Who? _____

What? _____

When? _____

Where? _____

Why? _____

DAILY TASKS

☐ Bible verse penmanship practice

☐ Practice your spelling words

☐ Individual reading time for 15-20 minutes

☐ Complete worksheets in your workbook

☐ Work on your unit art project or handicraft

BIBLE JOURNALING

Please write one sentence about something you learned that was meaningful to you from our Bible time today.

_____

_____

_____

_____

_____

_____

_____

_____

_____

Please practice writing this part of our memory verse.

Be still before the Lord and wait patiently for him.

Psalm 37:7

Pronoun are words that replace nouns. We are going to spend some more time practicing pronouns today. Please replace the underlined word or words with the proper pronoun.

Peter and John ran to see Jesus.
_____

_____

Hannah wanted a baby. God blessed Hannah with a baby boy.
_____

_____

My brother, my sister, and I all like to read the Bible.
_____

_____

It is Joseph's coat.
_____

_____

Please write a sentence using the word they and theirs.
_____

_____

Please write a sentence using the words we and our.
_____

_____

_____

DAILY TASKS

☐ Bible verse penmanship practice

☐ Practice your spelling words

☐ Individual reading time for 15-20 minutes

☐ Complete worksheets in your workbook

☐ History/Geography

MY DAY

Please fill in this information about your day.

DATE: _____ / _____ / _____

WEATHER

TIME: _____

Please draw a picture of something I read about from the Bible.

Please practice writing this part of our memory verse.

Be still before the Lord and wait patiently for him.

Psalm 37:7

BIBLE VERSE
MAPPING

- Write the definitions of the colored/underlined words by looking them up in a dictionary or online, write them next to the coordinating star. Include the part of speech.

- Circle the <u>nouns</u> in this passage.
- Underline the <u>verbs</u> in this passage.
- Box the <u>pronouns</u> in this passage.

"Yet a time is coming and has now come when the true worshipers will worship the Father in the Spirit and in <u>truth</u>, for they are the kind of worshipers the Father seeks. God is spirit, and his worshipers must worship in the Spirit and in truth." The woman said, "I know that Messiah" (called Christ) "is coming. When he comes, he will explain everything to us."
Then Jesus declared, "I, the one speaking to you—I am he."
John 4:23-26

★ _____
_____
_____
_____

CONTINENT STUDY
AFRICA

Today you are going to take the information you learned last week and make it into a poster report. Please include a picture of the continent, details about the population, size, and climate. Share your report with your family or friends and tell them about the continent you studied.

Population:

Size:

Climate:

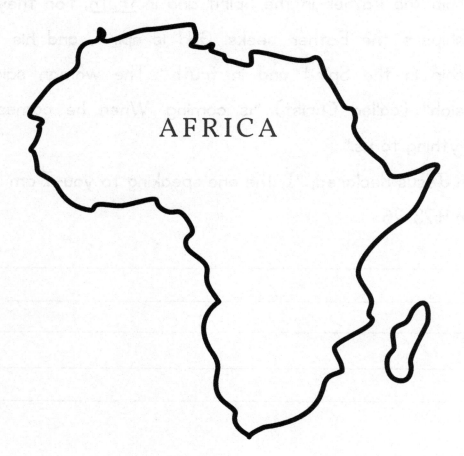

AFRICA

DAILY TASKS

☐ Bible verse penmanship practice

☐ Practice your spelling words

☐ Individual reading time for 15-20 minutes

☐ Complete worksheets in your workbook

☐ Science

BOOK SUMMARY

Please write a short summary of a book you have been reading for your individual reading time.

TITLE: _____

AUTHOR: _____

_____

_____

_____

_____

_____

Please practice writing this part of our memory verse.

<u>Be still before the Lord and wait patiently</u>
<u>for him.</u>

<u>Psalm 37:7</u>

SPELLING
PRACTICE

Please write each of your spelling words two times.

_____   _____

_____   _____

_____   _____

_____   _____

_____   _____

_____   _____

_____   _____

_____   _____

Please write two sentences using at least three of your spelling words.

_____

_____

_____

_____

_____

WATER CYCLE
SCIENCE WORKSHEET

Please label the parts of the water cycle.

_____   _____

_____   _____

_____   _____

_____   _____

DAILY TASKS

- ☐ Bible verse penmanship practice

- ☐ Spelling test

- ☐ Individual reading time for 15-20 minutes

- ☐ Complete worksheets in your workbook

- ☐ Check your work for the week, review anything that felt challenging

FACT OF THE WEEK

Please read this information. It is fun to learn new things!

ECOSYSTEMS

Marine

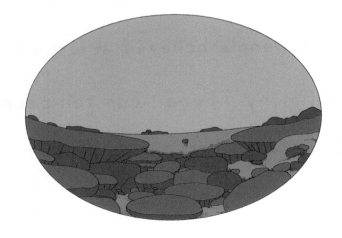

Aquatic environments characterized by high levels of dissolved salt.

EDITING
PRACTICE

Please look at the following story. Correct any mistakes in capitalization, and add any needed punctuation.

jesus had compassion for people. he loved the people and wanted them to be saved He is the Messiah, the Savior of the world. when jesus met the woman at the well he told her everything she ever did She went to tell others. i can tell people about jesus too! I can tell people that jesus loves them. i can tell people that Jesus died for their sins Many people believed in jesus because of the woman's testimony. i hope i can tell people about jesus and have them choose to follow him

HISTORICAL

PERSON OF INTEREST

Please choose a person you have learned about to answer these questions and write a report. You may need your parent to help you locate these facts using the internet or the book you have been reading. On the back please write one paragraph about this person.

1. Who are you learning about?

_____

_____

2. What did they do?

_____

_____

3. When did they live?

_____

_____

4. Where did they live?

_____

_____

5. Why would someone be interested in learning about this person?

_____

_____

_____

_____

_____

_____

_____

Write one paragraph about the person you have chosen. Be sure to include their name, why they are interesting, where they lived, and when they lived there. Imagine you are writing to someone who knows nothing about the person you are writing about.

<u>Paragraph Check List</u>

☐ Topic sentence

☐ Supporting sentences

☐ Closing sentence

☐ The 5 Ws

_____

_____

_____

_____

_____

_____

_____

_____

_____

_____

_____

_____

_____

_____

_____

 ## DAILY TASKS

☐ Bible verse penmanship practice

☐ Practice your spelling words

☐ Individual reading time for 15-20 minutes

☐ Complete worksheets in your workbook

☐ Work on your unit art project or handicraft

BIBLE JOURNALING

Please write one sentence about something you learned that was meaningful to you from our Bible time today.

_____

_____

_____

_____

_____

_____

_____

_____

Please draw a picture of something I read about from the Bible.

Please practice writing this part of our memory verse.

"'Love the Lord your God with all your heart and with all your soul and with all your mind.' This is the first and greatest commandment. And the second is like it: 'Love your neighbor as yourself.' "
Matthew 22:37-38

Plural means more than one. There are different rules for when we add "s" or "es" to the end of a noun to make it plural. There are also a few exceptions to the rule. We will practice more of these soon.

Please look at the following chart.

$$\begin{bmatrix} \text{a Bible} \\ \text{an apple} \end{bmatrix} + s \longrightarrow \begin{array}{l} \text{three Bibles} \\ \text{four apples} \end{array}$$

If a word ends in s, ss, sh, ch, or x we add es to make it plural.

$$\begin{bmatrix} \text{wish} \\ \text{batch} \\ \text{box} \end{bmatrix} + es = \begin{array}{l} \text{wishes} \\ \text{batches} \\ \text{boxes} \end{array}$$

Irregular	
man	two men
woman	three women
child	four children
person	five people

Please make these words plural by adding s or es to the end.

fox   test   teaching

mess   law   mom

latch   word   brush

Please write a sentence using the plural form of man and child.

_____

_____

_____

BIBLE VERSE
MAPPING

With the help of your parents, please choose a Bible verse from one of the chapters we read this week to verse map.

*Note to parents: Please review the grammar focus, and try to assist your child in choosing a passage that will contain multiple opportunities to practice this principle.

- Work with your parent to study this verse. Talk about what it means.

- Look up any words you do not understand.

Grammar Focus:

A verb is a word that shows action or state of being. Today we are going to work on words that show action.

Examples: run, sit, hop, make, running, talking, ate, walked, jumped

- Please underline all words that show action.
- Please circle all nouns in the verse you choose to write.
- Please star any proper nouns.
- Please box any pronouns

"Sing to the Lord with grateful praise; make music to our God on the harp. He covers the sky with clouds; he supplies the earth with rain and makes grass grow on the hills." Psalm 147:7-8

DAILY TASKS

☐ Bible verse penmanship practice

☐ Practice your spelling words

☐ Individual reading time for 15-20 minutes

☐ Complete worksheets in your workbook

☐ History/Geography

MY DAY

Please fill in this information about your day.

DATE: ___ / ___ / _____

WEATHER

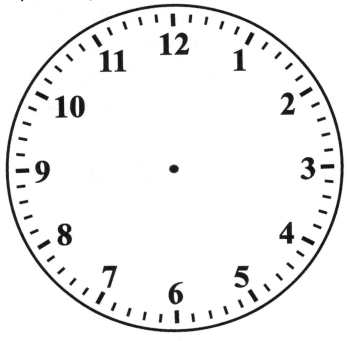

TIME: _____

95

Please practice writing this part of our memory verse.

"'Love the Lord your God with all your heart and with all your soul and with all your mind.' This is the first and greatest commandment. And the second is like it: 'Love your neighbor as yourself.' "
Matthew 22:37-38

COUNTRY STUDY

Have your parent help you get these answers from books or the internet.

Country to study:

_____

_____

Draw a photo of the countries flag

in the box provided.

1. What is the population?

_____

_____

2. What is the climate?

_____

_____

3. What are the 3 largest cities?

_____

_____

_____

4. Are people able to be Christians without persecution?

_____

_____

5. What is the primary source of income?

_____

_____

6. How is their government structured?

_____

_____

7. What is the main people group? What is the main language spoken?

_____

DAILY TASKS

☐ Bible verse penmanship practice

☐ Practice your spelling words

☐ Individual reading time for 15-20 minutes

☐ Complete worksheets in your workbook

☐ Science 💡

JOURNALING MY WEEK

Please write 1-2 sentences about your week. You may choose to tell something you have learned, done, or experienced.

_____

_____

_____

_____

_____

_____

_____

_____

_____

Please draw a picture of something I read about from the Bible.

Please practice writing this part of our memory verse.

"'Love the Lord your God with all your heart and with all your soul and with all your mind.' This is the first and greatest commandment. And the second is like it: 'Love your neighbor as yourself.' "
Matthew 22:37-38

SPELLING
PRACTICE

Please write each of your spelling words two times.

_____   _____

_____   _____

_____   _____

_____   _____

_____   _____

_____   _____

_____   _____

WRITE A LETTER

*Parents: Help your child write a properly formatted letter including a greeting, body, closing, and signature. (If you struggle to remember this look up "personal letter format". Don't forget to add any misspelled words to your child's spelling list. Explain placement of the address, return address, and stamp. Tell your child the price of a stamp.

Please write a letter to a friend or family member. Have your parent edit your letter. Correct any mistakes in spelling or grammar.

Address the envelope for your letter and put your return address with the help of your parent. Each time you send a letter you will get more confident in this. Use good penmanship so the post office can easily read what you wrote.

CLOUDS
SCIENCE WORKSHEET

Match the clouds with their proper definition.

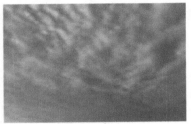

stratus

cirrus

cumulus

cumulonimbus

stratocumulus

White,

feathery,

highest

Wide blankets

of gray "high fog"

Gray, low in

the sky, lumpy

Puffy, flat bottoms,

low in the sky

Thunderstorms

clouds, look likes

mountains

of very tall

cumulus clouds

DAILY TASKS

☐ Bible verse penmanship practice

☐ Spelling test

☐ Individual reading time for 15-20 minutes

☐ Complete worksheets in your workbook

☐ Check your work for the week, review anything that felt challenging

FACT OF THE WEEK

Please read this information. It is fun to learn new things!

ECOSYSTEMS

Tundra

Treeless environments with low temperatures and low rainfall.

EDITING
PRACTICE

Please look at the following story. Correct any mistakes in capitalization and add any needed punctuation.

jesus had compassion for people. he loved the people and wanted them to be saved He is the Messiah, the Savior of the world. when jesus met the woman at the well he told her everything she ever did She went to tell others. i can tell people about jesus too! I can tell people that jesus loves them. i can tell people that Jesus died for their sins Many people believed in jesus because of the woman's testimony. i hope i can tell people about jesus and have them choose to follow him

STORIES FROM SCRIPTURE
WRITING PROJECT

Please choose one of the stories we have read from the Bible this week to write about. Imagine you are telling the story to someone who has never heard it. Tell them why you like this story and what it means to you. Answer the 5 W questions to help you write. Use additional notebook paper if needed.

Who? _____

What? _____

When? _____

Where? _____

Why? _____

_____

_____

_____

_____

_____

_____

_____

DAILY TASKS

☐ Bible verse penmanship practice

☐ Practice your spelling words

☐ Individual reading time for 15-20 minutes

☐ Complete worksheets in your workbook

☐ Work on your unit art project or handicraft

BIBLE JOURNALING

Please write one sentence about something you learned that was meaningful to you from our Bible time today.

_____

_____

_____

_____

_____

_____

_____

_____

Please draw a picture of something I read about from the Bible.

Please practice writing this part of our memory verse.

<u>Now faith is confidence in what we hope for</u>
<u>and assurance about what we do not see.</u>
<u>Hebrews 11:1</u>

Quotations:

There are various different times we use quotation marks within a sentence. Today we are going to practice showing that someone is speaking.

Example: In Genesis chapter one God said, "Let there be light," and then there was light.

We put a comma before the quote begins, and keep all punctuation within the quote.

Please write Mark 2:5 using the correct punctuation for the quote. Who is speaking in this sentence? _____

_____

_____

_____

_____

_____

_____

DAILY TASKS

☐ Bible verse penmanship practice

☐ Practice your spelling words

☐ Individual reading time for 15-20 minutes

☐ Complete worksheets in your workbook

☐ History/Geography 🕐 🌐

MY DAY

Please fill in this information about your day.

DATE: ___ / ___ / ___

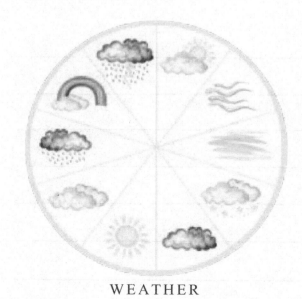

WEATHER

TIME: _____

Please practice writing this part of our memory verse.

Now faith is confidence in what we hope for and assurance about what we do not see. Hebrews 11:1

COUNTRY STUDY

We are going to use the information you gathered last week to choose a project to do on the country you chose to study. You have options to choose from. Please work with your parent to choose one that will work best for you.

1. Make a photo collage/information poster like we did for our continent study. Remember to include valuable information. Present this to your family or friends and share with them interesting facts you learned about this country.

2. Make a traditional food from the country you are studying. You will need help from your parents with this. Serve the food to your family and share about the country it originates from.

3. Write a report about Christians in the country you chose. Include details about missions, persecution, laws, and family pressure. Include names of prominent missionaries or evangelists. Include the history of Christianity and the current state of the Church.

Project choice
_____
_____

What is needed for your project?
_____
_____
_____

Have fun and do your best!

_____

Please write the name of the country you have chosen.

Draw a picture of the country.

Please write some interesting facts your learn about this country. Include some details about how they live and what they eat.

_____

_____

_____

_____

_____

_____

DAILY TASKS

☐ Bible verse penmanship practice

☐ Practice your spelling words

☐ Individual reading time for 15-20 minutes

☐ Complete worksheets in your workbook

☐ Science

BOOK SUMMARY

Please write a short summary of a book you have been reading for your individual reading time.

TITLE: _____

AUTHOR: _____

_____

_____

_____

_____

_____

Please draw a picture of something I read about from the Bible.

Please practice writing this part of our memory verse.

Now faith is confidence in what we hope for and assurance about what we do not see. Hebrews 11:1

SPELLING
PRACTICE

Please write each of your spelling words two times.

_____   _____

_____   _____

_____   _____

_____   _____

_____   _____

_____   _____

_____   _____

Please write two sentences using at least three of your spelling words.

_____

_____

_____

_____

_____

_____

WATER SYSTEM
SCIENCE ACTIVITY

Please choose a lake, river, or ocean near your home to draw a picture of. You may choose a small section. Please highlight specific types of plants and include their names. Also include names and photos of wildlife, fish, and insects you would expect to see in the area you chose. All of the elements of a particular area is called an ecosystem.

DAILY TASKS

☐ Bible verse penmanship practice

☐ Spelling test

☐ Individual reading time for 15-20 minutes

☐ Complete worksheets in your workbook

☐ Check your work for the week, review anything that felt challenging

FACT OF THE WEEK

Please read this information. It is fun to learn new things!

AMAZING ADAPTATIONS OF ANIMALS

God created animals in a way that helps them to survive in their habitats through adaptation. This means that they have certain traits that help them to survive in the environment in which they live! The world may try to present this in a way that supports evolution, but we know that it is possible by God's design!

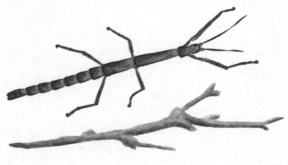

BIBLE VERSE

MAPPING

>>>>>>>>> <<<<<<<<<

- Please look at this verse in your Bible and add the quotation marks where needed.
- Define the underlined word.

Jesus stepped into a boat, crossed over and came to his own town. Some men brought to him a **paralyzed** man, lying on a mat. When Jesus saw their <u>faith</u>, he said to the man,

Take heart, son; your sins are forgiven.

At this, some of the teachers of the law said to themselves,

This fellow is blaspheming!

Matthew 9:1-2

★ _____

_____

_____

_____

HISTORICAL
PERSON OF INTEREST

Please choose a person you have learned about to answer these questions and write a report. You may need your parent to help you locate these facts using the internet or the book you have been reading. On the back please write one paragraph about this person.

1. Who are you learning about?
_____
_____

2. What did they do?
_____
_____

3. When did they live?
_____
_____

4. Where did they live?
_____
_____

5. Why would someone be interested in learning about this person?
_____
_____
_____
_____
_____
_____
_____

Write one paragraph about the person you have chosen. Be sure to include their name, why they are interesting, where they lived, and when they lived there. Imagine you are writing to someone who knows nothing about the person you are writing about.

<u>Paragraph Check List</u>

☐ Topic sentence

☐ Supporting sentences

☐ Closing sentence

☐ The 5 Ws

_____

_____

_____

_____

_____

_____

_____

_____

_____

_____

_____

_____

_____

_____

CREATE YOUR OWN MINI UNIT STUDY

This week you will create a mini-unit study on something you wish to study. Work with your parent to come up with ideas and a plan.

Topic of Study: _____

List of ways to learn about this topic:

_____
_____
_____
_____
_____
_____

Scriptures that apply:

_____
_____
_____
_____

Field trip or activity ideas:

_____
_____
_____
_____
_____

CREATE YOUR OWN MINI UNIT STUDY

Draw a picture of your topic of choice:

UNIT

three

UNIT three

SPELLING LISTS

Your student's spelling words will come from words you identify that they spell incorrectly in their writing. As your student writes for assignments (or any other writing) please write the words they spell incorrectly here. At the end of the week there will be a spelling quiz. If your student continues to struggle with a word add it to the following week's list.

Week 1	Week 2	Week 3	Week 4

DAILY TASKS

☐ Bible verse penmanship practice

☐ Practice your spelling words

☐ Individual reading time for 15-20 minutes

☐ Complete worksheets in your workbook

☐ Work on your unit art project or handicraft

BIBLE JOURNALING

Please write one sentence about something you learned that was meaningful to you from our Bible time today.

_____

_____

_____

_____

_____

_____

_____

_____

_____

Please draw a picture of something I read about from the Bible.

Please practice writing this part of our memory verse.

"Have I not commanded you? Be strong and courageous. Do not be afraid; do not be discouraged, for the Lord your God will be with you wherever you go."

Joshua 1:9

BIBLE VERSE
GRAMMAR PRACTICE

>>>>>>>>>> BIBLE VERSE <<<<<<<<<<

Please circle the homophones in the following Bible verses and write the homophone set.

"Know that the LORD is God. It is he who made us, and we are his; we are his people, the sheep of his pasture." Psalm 100:3

"For the Lord God is a sun and shield; the Lord bestows favor and honor; no good thing does he withhold from those whose walk is blameless." Psalm 84:11

Homophone set: _____

"Lift up your eyes and see. Who has made these stars? It is the One Who leads them out by number. He calls them all by name. Because of the greatness of His strength, and because He is strong in power, not one of them is missing." Isaiah 40:26

"Then Moses stretched out his hand over the sea, and all that night the LORD drove the sea back with a strong east wind and turned it into dry land. The waters were divided." Exodus 14:21

Homophone set: _____

DAILY TASKS

☐ Bible verse penmanship practice

☐ Practice your spelling words

☐ Individual reading time for 15-20 minutes

☐ Complete worksheets in your workbook

☐ History/Geography

MY DAY

Please fill in this information about your day.

DATE: ___ / ___ / ___

WEATHER

TIME: _____

Please practice writing this part of our memory verse.

"Be strong and courageous. Do not be afraid; do not be discouraged, for the Lord your God will be with you wherever you go."

Joshua 1:9

CONTINENT STUDY
ASIA

Work with your parent to get these answers from books or the internet.

1. Where is this continent located? What hemisphere(s) is it in?

_____

_____

2. What is the climate?

_____

_____

3. What oceans are near this continent?

_____

_____

4. How many countries are on this continent?

_____

_____

5. What is the population?

_____

_____

6. How large is this continent?

_____

_____

7. What are the top natural resources?

_____

_____

8. What are the main religions?

_____

_____

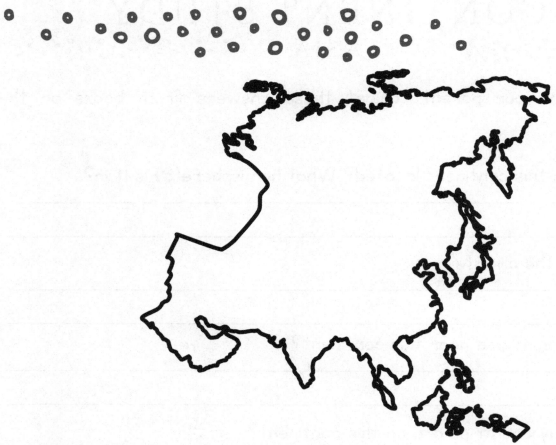

- Please label the 3 largest cities. Use a red dot to mark.

- Draw in any major rivers or lakes with blue colored pencil.

- If the equator crosses this continent, please draw a black line to show where.

- Please label the oceans around this continent.

Name of this continent:

_____

_____

We will study one country from this continent. Please choose which country you would like to study, and find resources to learn more about this country.

Country:

_____

_____

DAILY TASKS

☐ Bible verse penmanship practice

☐ Practice your spelling words

☐ Individual reading time for 15-20 minutes

☐ Complete worksheets in your workbook

☐ Science 💡

JOURNALING MY WEEK

Please write 1-2 sentences about your week. You may choose to tell something you have learned, done, or experienced.

_____

_____

_____

_____

_____

_____

_____

_____

Please practice writing this part of our memory verse.

"Be strong and courageous. Do not be afraid; do not be discouraged, for the Lord your God will be with you wherever you go."

Joshua 1:9

ACCORDING TO THEIR KIND
SCIENCE WORKSHEET

Please draw a picture of the seed from each fruit and label.

Fruit: _____

Fruit: _____

Fruit: _____

SPELLING
PRACTICE

Please write each of your spelling words two times.

_____   _____

_____   _____

_____   _____

_____   _____

_____   _____

_____   _____

Please write two sentences using at least three of your spelling words.

_____

_____

_____

_____

_____

_____

DAILY TASKS

☐ Bible verse penmanship practice

☐ Spelling test

☐ Individual reading time for 15-20 minutes

☐ Complete worksheets in your workbook

☐ Check your work for the week, review anything that felt challenging

FACT OF THE WEEK

Please read this information. It is fun to learn new things!

Because of its changing skin color, the chameleon can camouflage itself from predators.

STORIES FROM SCRIPTURE
WRITING PROJECT

Please choose one of the stories we have read from the Bible this week to write about. Imagine you are telling the story to someone who has never heard it. Tell them why you like this story and what it means to you. Answer the 5 W questions to help you write at least one paragraph. Use notebook paper to write, or type your paper on the computer. When you are finished writing, edit your work. Check for complete sentences, proper capitalization, and punctuation. Have your parent offer suggestions for ways to improve your writing. Be sure they edit for spelling. Add any words that are incorrect to next week's spelling list.

Who? _____

What? _____

When? _____

Where? _____

Why? _____

DAILY TASKS

☐ Bible verse penmanship practice

☐ Practice your spelling words

☐ Individual reading time for 15-20 minutes

☐ Complete worksheets in your workbook

☐ Work on your unit art project or handicraft

BIBLE JOURNALING

Please write one sentence about something you learned that was meaningful to you from our Bible time today.

_____

_____

_____

_____

_____

_____

_____

_____

_____

Please practice writing this part of our memory verse.

"Does the Lord delight in burnt offerings and sacrifice as much as in obeying the Lord? To obey is better than sacrifice, and to heed is better than the fat of rams."

I Samuel 15:22

EDITING
PRACTICE

Please look at the following Bible verses. Correct any mistakes in capitalization and add any needed punctuation, including quotation marks.

and there were shepherds living out in the fields nearby, keeping watch over their flocks at night An angel of the Lord appeared to them, and the glory of the lord shone around them, and they were terrified. But the angel said to them, Do not be afraid. I bring you good news that will cause great joy for all the people. today in the town of David a Savior has been born to you; he is the Messiah, the Lord. this will be a sign to you: You will find a baby wrapped in cloths and lying in a manger.

luke 2:8-12

 DAILY TASKS

☐ Bible verse penmanship practice

☐ Practice your spelling words

☐ Individual reading time for 15-20 minutes

☐ Complete worksheets in your workbook

☐ History/Geography

MY DAY

Please fill in this information about your day.

DATE: ___ / ___ / ___

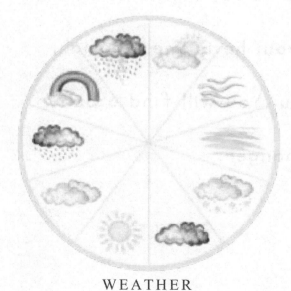

WEATHER

TIME: _____

Please draw a picture of something I read about from the Bible.

Please practice writing this part of our memory verse.

"To obey is better than sacrifice, and to heed is better than the fat of rams."

I Samuel 15:22b

CONTINENT STUDY
ASIA

Today you are going to take the information you learned last week and make it into a poster report. Please include a picture of the continent, details about the population, size, and climate. Share your report with your family or friends and tell them about the continent you studied.

Population:

Size:

Climate:

WEEK 2, DAY 3

DAILY TASKS

- ☐ Bible verse penmanship practice

- ☐ Practice your spelling words

- ☐ Individual reading time for 15-20 minutes

- ☐ Complete worksheets in your workbook

- ☐ Science

BOOK SUMMARY

Please write a short summary of a book you have been reading for your individual reading time.

TITLE: _____

AUTHOR: _____

_____

_____

_____

_____

_____

God hears us when we pray

Please practice writing this part of our memory verse.

"To obey is better than sacrifice, and to heed is better than the fat of rams."

I Samuel 15:22b

SPELLING
PRACTICE

Please write each of your spelling words two times.

_____   _____

_____   _____

_____   _____

_____   _____

_____   _____

_____   _____

_____   _____

_____   _____

_____   _____

_____   _____

Please write two sentences using at least three of your spelling words.

_____

_____

_____

_____

_____

CYCLE OF A PLANT
SCIENCE WORKSHEET

_____

_____

_____

_____

LIFE CYCLE
OF A PEA

_____

_____

_____

_____

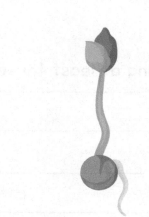

_____

_____

_____

_____

Please label each stage

DAILY TASKS

☐ Bible verse penmanship practice

☐ Spelling test

☐ Individual reading time for 15-20 minutes

☐ Complete worksheets in your workbook

☐ Check your work for the week, review anything that felt challenging

FACT OF THE WEEK

Please read this information. It is fun to learn new things!

GIRAFFE

The giraffe's long neck allows it exclusive access to food.

HISTORICAL

PERSON OF INTEREST

Please choose a person you have learned about to answer these questions and write a report. You may need your parent to help you locate these facts using the internet or the book you have been reading. On the back please write two to three paragraphs about this person.

1. Who are you learning about?

_____

_____

2. What did they do?

_____

_____

3. When did they live?

_____

_____

4. Where did they live?

_____

_____

5. Why would someone be interested in learning about this person?

_____

_____

_____

_____

_____

_____

Write one paragraph about the person you have chosen. Be sure to include their name, why they are interesting, where they lived, and when they lived there. Imagine you are writing to someone who knows nothing about the person you are writing about.

<u>Paragraph Check List</u>

☐ Topic sentence

☐ Supporting sentences

☐ Closing sentence

☐ The 5 Ws

_____

_____

_____

_____

_____

_____

_____

_____

_____

_____

_____

_____

_____

DAILY TASKS

☐ Bible verse penmanship practice

☐ Practice your spelling words

☐ Individual reading time for 15-20 minutes

☐ Complete worksheets in your workbook

☐ Work on your unit art project or handicraft

BIBLE JOURNALING

Please write one sentence about something you learned that was meaningful to you from our Bible time today.

_____

_____

_____

_____

_____

_____

_____

_____

Please draw a picture of something I read about from the Bible.

Please practice writing this part of our memory verse.

"But be sure to fear the Lord and serve him faithfully with all your heart."

I Samuel 12:24a

BIBLE VERSE
GRAMMAR PRACTICE

Please circle the homonyms in the following Bible verses and write the meaning of both uses of this word. (You may use a dictionary or write your own definition if you feel you are able to do so.)

"Do not turn to the right or the left; keep your foot from evil."
Proverbs 4:27

"If you do what is right, will you not be accepted? But if you do not do what is right, sin is crouching at your door; it desires to have you, but you must rule over it."
Genesis 4:7

Word: _____

Definition 1: _____

_____

_____

_____

Definition 2: _____

_____

_____

_____

DAILY TASKS

☐ Bible verse penmanship practice

☐ Practice your spelling words

☐ Individual reading time for 15-20 minutes

☐ Complete worksheets in your workbook

☐ History/Geography

MY DAY

Please fill in this information about your day.

DATE: _____ / _____ / _____

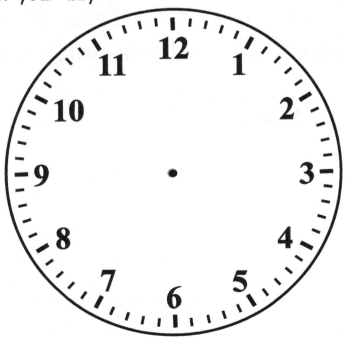

WEATHER

TIME: _____

Please practice writing this part of our memory verse.

"But be sure to fear the Lord and serve him faithfully with all your heart."

I Samuel 12:24a

COUNTRY STUDY

Have your parent help you get these answers from books or the internet.

Country to study:

_____

_____

Draw a photo of the country's flag
in the box provided.

1. What is the population?

_____

_____

2. What is the climate?

_____

_____

3. What are the 3 largest cities?

_____

_____

_____

_____

4. Are people able to be Christians without persecution?

_____

5. What is the primary source of income?

_____

6. How is their government structured?

_____

7. What is the main people group? What is the main language spoken?

_____

DAILY TASKS

☐ Bible verse penmanship practice

☐ Practice your spelling words

☐ Individual reading time for 15-20 minutes

☐ Complete worksheets in your workbook

☐ Science 💡

JOURNALING MY WEEK

Please write 1-2 sentences about your week. You may choose to tell something you have learned, done, or experienced.

_____

_____

_____

_____

_____

_____

_____

_____

_____

Please draw a picture of something I read about from the Bible.

Please practice writing this part of our memory verse.

"But be sure to fear the Lord and serve him
faithfully with all your heart."

I Samuel 12:24a

SPELLING
PRACTICE

Please write each of your spelling words two times.

_____   _____

_____   _____

_____   _____

_____   _____

_____   _____

_____   _____

_____   _____

WRITE A LETTER

*Parents: Help your child write a properly formatted letter including a greeting, body, closing, and signature. (If you struggle to remember this look up "personal letter format". Don't forget to add any misspelled words to your child's spelling list. Explain placement of the address, return address, and stamp. Tell your child the price of a stamp.

Please write a letter to a friend or family member. Have your parent edit your letter. Correct any mistakes in spelling or grammar.

Address the envelope for your letter and put your return address with the help of your parent. Each time you send a letter you will get more confident in this. Use good penmanship so the post office can easily read what you wrote.

PARTS OF A PLANT
SCIENCE WORKSHEET

Please label the parts of a plant.

_____

_____

DAILY TASKS

☐ Bible verse penmanship practice

☐ Spelling test

☐ Individual reading time for 15-20 minutes

☐ Complete worksheets in your workbook

☐ Check your work for the week, review anything that felt challenging

FACT OF THE WEEK

Please read this information. It is fun to learn new things!

CAMEL

Camels survive in dry, arid conditions as it stores fat in its humps which allows for better regulation of its body temperature.

 REVIEW

Please draw a line from each part of speech to its proper definition.

describes a noun

Noun

replaces a proper

Verb   noun

Pronoun   a person, place, or

thing

Adjective

shows action

Please write the abbreviations for the following words.

Doctor _____

Missus _____

Mister _____

Monday _____

STORIES FROM SCRIPTURE
WRITING PROJECT

Please choose one of the stories we have read from the Bible this week to write about. Imagine you are telling the story to someone who has never heard it. Tell them why you like this story and what it means to you. Answer the 5 W questions to help you write. Use additional notebook paper if needed.

Who? _____

What? _____

When? _____

Where? _____

Why? _____

_____

_____

_____

_____

_____

_____

_____

_____

DAILY TASKS

☐ Bible verse penmanship practice

☐ Practice your spelling words

☐ Individual reading time for 15-20 minutes

☐ Complete worksheets in your workbook

☐ Work on your unit art project or handicraft

BIBLE JOURNALING

Please write one sentence about something you learned that was meaningful to you from our Bible time today.

_____

_____

_____

_____

_____

_____

_____

_____

_____

Please draw a picture of something I read about from the Bible.

Please practice writing this part of our memory verse.

"Answer me, Lord, answer me, so these people will know that you, Lord, are God, and that you are turning their hearts back again."

I Kings 18:37

Please define the underlined word.

"Jesus stepped into a boat, crossed over and came to his own town. Some men brought to him a <u>paralyzed</u> man, lying on a mat. When Jesus saw their faith, he said to the man, Take heart, son; your sins are forgiven.

At this, some of the teachers of the law said to themselves, This fellow is blaspheming!"

Matthew 9:1-2

★ _____

_____

_____

_____

DAILY TASKS

☐ Bible verse penmanship practice

☐ Practice your spelling words

☐ Individual reading time for 15-20 minutes

☐ Complete worksheets in your workbook

☐ History/Geography

MY DAY

Please fill in this information about your day.

DATE: _____ / ____ / _____

WEATHER

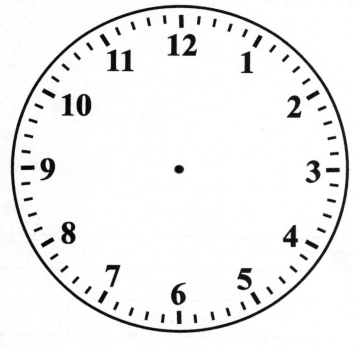

TIME: _____

166

Please practice writing this part of our memory verse.

"Answer me, Lord, answer me, so these people will know that you, Lord, are God, and that you are turning their hearts back again."

1 Kings 18:37

COUNTRY STUDY

We are going to use the information you gathered last week to choose a project to do on the country you chose to study. You have options to choose from. Please work with your parent to choose one that will work best for you.

1. Make a photo collage/information poster like we did for our continent study. Remember to include valuable information. Present this to your family or friends and share with them interesting facts you learned about this country.

2. Make a traditional food from the country you are studying. You will need help from your parents with this. Serve the food to your family and share about the country it originates from.

3. Write a report about Christians in the country you chose. Include details about missions, persecution, laws, and family pressure. Include names of prominent missionaries or evangelists. Include the history of Christianity and the current state of the Church.

Project choice

_____

_____

What is needed for your project?

_____

_____

Have fun and do your best!

_____

Please write the name of the country you have chosen.

Draw a picture of the country.

Please write some interesting facts your learn about this country. Include some details about how they live and what they eat.

_____

_____

_____

_____

_____

169

 DAILY TASKS

☐ Bible verse penmanship practice

☐ Practice your spelling words

☐ Individual reading time for 15-20 minutes

☐ Complete worksheets in your workbook

☐ Science

BOOK SUMMARY

Please write a short summary of a book you have been reading for your individual reading time.

TITLE: _____

AUTHOR: _____

_____

_____

_____

_____

_____

Please draw a picture of something I read about from the Bible.

Please practice writing this part of our memory verse.

"Answer me, Lord, answer me, so these people will know that you, Lord, are God, and that you are turning their hearts back again."

I Kings 18:37

SPELLING
PRACTICE

Please write each of your spelling words two times.

_____   _____

_____   _____

_____   _____

_____   _____

_____   _____

_____   _____

Please write two sentences using at least three of your spelling words.

_____

_____

_____

_____

_____

LAYERS OF SOIL
SCIENCE WORKSHEET

Please label the layers of soil.

_____

_____

_____

_____

_____

DAILY TASKS

☐ Bible verse penmanship practice

☐ Spelling test

☐ Individual reading time for 15-20 minutes

☐ Complete worksheets in your workbook

☐ Check your work for the week, review anything that felt challenging

FACT OF THE WEEK

Please read this information. It is fun to learn new things!

PEACOCK

The male peacock spreads its brightly colored tail to attract a mate.

HISTORICAL

PERSON OF INTEREST

Please choose a person you have learned about to answer these questions and write a report. You may need your parent to help you locate these facts using the internet or the book you have been reading. On the back, please write two to three paragraphs about this person.

1. Who are you learning about?

_____

_____

2. What did they do?

_____

_____

3. When did they live?

_____

_____

4. Where did they live?

_____

_____

5. Why would someone be interested in learning about this person?

_____

_____

_____

_____

_____

_____

_____

Write one paragraph about the person you have chosen. Be sure to include their name, why they are interesting, where they lived, and when they lived there. Imagine you are writing to someone who knows nothing about the person you are writing about.

<u>Paragraph Check List</u>

☐ Topic sentence

☐ Supporting sentences

☐ Closing sentence

☐ The 5 Ws

_____

_____

_____

_____

_____

_____

_____

_____

_____

_____

_____

_____

_____

_____

_____

CREATE YOUR OWN MINI UNIT STUDY

This week you will create a mini-unit study on something you wish to study. Work with your parent to come up with ideas and a plan.

Topic of Study: _____

List of ways to learn about this topic:

_____

_____

_____

_____

_____

_____

Scriptures that apply:

_____

_____

_____

Field trip or activity ideas:

_____

_____

_____

_____

UNIT
Four

UNIT
Four

SPELLING LISTS

Your student's spelling words will come from words you identify that they spell incorrectly in their writing. As your student writes for assignments (or any other writing) please write the words they spell incorrectly here. At the end of the week there will be a spelling quiz. If your student continues to struggle with a word add it to the following week's list.

Week 1	Week 2	Week 3	Week 4

WEEK 1, DAY 1

DAILY TASKS

☐ Bible verse penmanship practice

☐ Practice your spelling words

☐ Individual reading time for 15-20 minutes

☐ Complete worksheets in your workbook

☐ Work on your unit art project or handicraft

BIBLE JOURNALING

Please write one sentence about something you learned that was meaningful to you from our Bible time today.

_____

_____

_____

_____

_____

_____

_____

_____

_____

Please draw a picture of something I read about from the Bible.

Please practice writing this part of our memory verse.

"Blessed are the poor in spirit,
for theirs is the kingdom of heaven"

Matthew 5:3

EDITING
PRACTICE

Please look at the following story and correct any mistakes in capitalization and punctuation. Remember, days of the week, months, and proper nouns are all capitalized.

john is planning a party for his birthday His birthday is on Wednesday, october 15. he is planning his birthday for the Friday after his birthday so his grandparents can make it to his party John plans to have his friends joe tom, and paul come to his party also. john's mom, sandy, is making his cake. His sister lucy is making him a special gift She hopes to finish the surprise before his party

DAILY TASKS

☐ Bible verse penmanship practice

☐ Practice your spelling words

☐ Individual reading time for 15-20 minutes

☐ Complete worksheets in your workbook

☐ History/Geography

MY DAY

Please fill in this information about your day.

DATE: _____ / _____ / _____

WEATHER

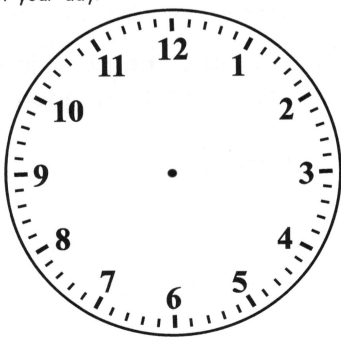

TIME: _____

Please practice writing this part of our memory verse.

"Blessed are the poor in spirit,
for theirs is the kingdom of heaven"

Matthew 5:3

CONTINENT STUDY
AUSTRALIA/OCEANIA

Work with your parent to get these answers from books or the internet.

1. Where is this continent located? What hemisphere(s) is it in?

_____

_____

2. What is the climate?

_____

_____

3. What oceans are near this continent?

_____

_____

4. How many countries are on this continent?

_____

_____

5. What is the population?

_____

_____

6. How large is this continent?

_____

_____

7. What are the top natural resources?

_____

_____

8. What are the main religions?

_____

_____

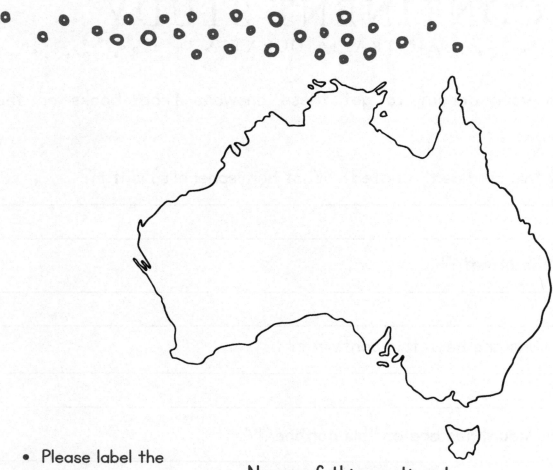

- Please label the 3 largest cities, use a red dot to mark.
- Draw in any major rivers or lakes with blue colored pencil
- If the equator crosses this continent please draw a black line to show where.
- Please label the oceans around this continent.

Name of this continent:

_____

_____

We will study one country from this continent. Please choose which country you would like to study and find resources to learn more about this country.

Country:

_____

_____

DAILY TASKS

☐ Bible verse penmanship practice

☐ Practice your spelling words

☐ Individual reading time for 15-20 minutes

☐ Complete worksheets in your workbook

☐ Science 💡

JOURNALING MY WEEK

Please write 1-2 sentences about your week. You may choose to tell something you have learned, done, or experienced.

_____

_____

_____

_____

_____

_____

_____

_____

_____

Please practice writing this part of our memory verse.

"Blessed are the poor in spirit,
for theirs is the kingdom of heaven"

Matthew 5:3

 # MOON PHASE
SCIENCE WORKSHEET

Over the next month, please record what date you see each of these phases occur.

Full Moon:

Waxing Gibeous:

Waning Gibeous:

First Quarter:

Third Quarter:

Waxing Cresent:

Waning Cresent:

New Moon:

SPELLING
PRACTICE

Please write each of your spelling words two times.

_____   _____

_____   _____

_____   _____

_____   _____

_____   _____

_____   _____

Please write two sentences using at least three of your spelling words.

_____

_____

_____

_____

_____

WEEK 1, DAY 4

DAILY TASKS

☐ Bible verse penmanship practice

☐ Spelling test

☐ Individual reading time for 15-20 minutes

☐ Complete worksheets in your workbook

☐ Check your work for the week, review anything that felt challenging

FACT OF THE WEEK

Please read this information. It is fun to learn new things!

Electricity

Energy created when electrons move from one atom to another.

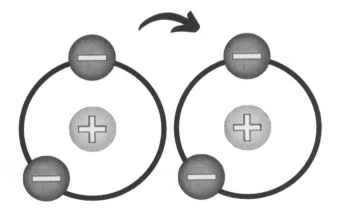

Want to learn more about the history of electricity? Study Benjamin Franklin!

STORIES FROM SCRIPTURE
WRITING PROJECT

Please choose one of the stories we have read from the Bible this week to write about. Imagine you are telling the story to someone who has never heard it. Tell them why you like this story and what it means to you. Answer the 5 W questions to help you write. Use additional notebook paper if needed.

Who? _____

What? _____

When? _____

Where? _____

Why? _____

_____

_____

_____

_____

_____

_____

DAILY TASKS

☐ Bible verse penmanship practice

☐ Practice your spelling words

☐ Individual reading time for 15-20 minutes

☐ Complete worksheets in your workbook

☐ Work on your unit art project or handicraft

BIBLE JOURNALING

Please write one sentence about something you learned that was meaningful to you from our Bible time today.

_____

_____

_____

_____

_____

_____

_____

_____

Please practice writing this part of our memory verse.

"Blessed are those who hunger and thirst for righteousness, for they will be filled."

Matthew 5:6

DAILY TASKS

☐ Bible verse penmanship practice

☐ Practice your spelling words

☐ Individual reading time for 15-20 minutes

☐ Complete worksheets in your workbook

☐ History/Geography

MY DAY

Please fill in this information about your day.

DATE: ___ / ___ / ___

WEATHER

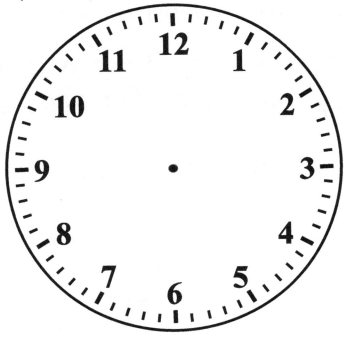

TIME: _____

Please draw a picture of something I read about from the Bible.

Please practice writing this part of our memory verse.

"Blessed are those who hunger and thirst for righteousness, for they will be filled."

Matthew 5:6

CONTINENT STUDY
AUSTRALIA

Today you are going to take the information you learned last week and make it into a poster report. Please include a picture of the continent, details about the population, size, and climate. Share your report with your family or friends and tell them about the continent you studied.

Population:

Size:

Climate:

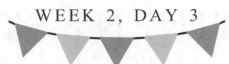

 DAILY TASKS

☐ Bible verse penmanship practice

☐ Practice your spelling words

☐ Individual reading time for 15-20 minutes

☐ Complete worksheets in your workbook

☐ Science 🔅

BOOK SUMMARY

Please write a short summary of a book you have been reading for your individual reading time.

TITLE: _____

AUTHOR: _____

_____

_____

_____

_____

_____

Please practice writing this part of our memory verse.

"Blessed are those who hunger and thirst for righteousness, for they will be filled."

Matthew 5:6

Please write each of your spelling words two times.

_____   _____

_____   _____

_____   _____

_____   _____

_____   _____

_____   _____

_____   _____

Please write two sentences using at least three of your spelling words.

_____

_____

_____

_____

_____

CONSTELLATIONS
SCIENCE WORKSHEET

Please label these constellations and build models out of grapes and toothpicks. See if you can locate these tonight in the sky!

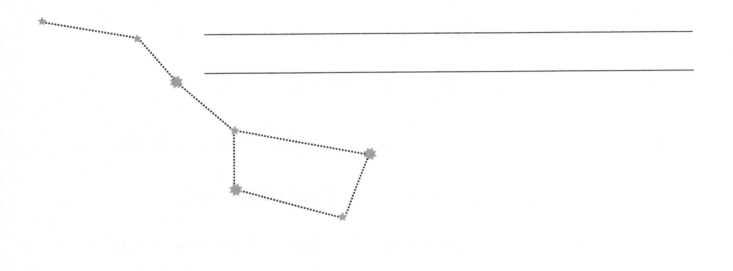

_____

_____

_____

_____

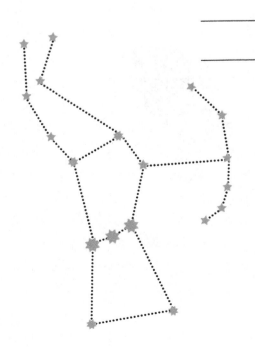

DAILY TASKS

☐ Bible verse penmanship practice

☐ Spelling test

☐ Individual reading time for 15-20 minutes

☐ Complete worksheets in your workbook

☐ Check your work for the week, review anything that felt challenging

FACT OF THE WEEK

Please read this information. It is fun to learn new things!

Static Electricity

produced when two objects are rubbed together, creating friction

HISTORICAL
PERSON OF INTEREST

Please choose a person you have learned about to answer these questions and write a report. You may need your parent to help you locate these facts using the internet or the book you have been reading. On the back, please write two to three paragraphs about this person.

1. Who are you learning about?

_____

_____

2. What did they do?

_____

_____

3. When did they live?

_____

_____

4. Where did they live?

_____

_____

5. Why would someone be interested in learning about this person?

_____

_____

_____

_____

_____

_____

_____

Write one paragraph about the person you have chosen. Be sure to include their name, why they are interesting, where they lived, and when they lived there. Imagine you are writing to someone who knows nothing about the person you are writing about.

<u>Paragraph Check List</u>

☐ Topic sentence
☐ Supporting sentences
☐ Closing sentence
☐ The 5 Ws

_____
_____
_____
_____
_____
_____
_____
_____
_____
_____
_____
_____
_____
_____
_____

DAILY TASKS

☐ Bible verse penmanship practice

☐ Practice your spelling words

☐ Individual reading time for 15-20 minutes

☐ Complete worksheets in your workbook

☐ Work on your unit art project or handicraft

BIBLE JOURNALING

Please write one sentence about something you learned that was meaningful to you from our Bible time today.

_____

_____

_____

_____

_____

_____

_____

_____

_____

Please draw a picture of something I read about from the Bible.

Please practice writing this part of our memory verse.

"Blessed are the merciful,
for they will be shown mercy."

Matthew 5:7

BIBLE VERSE

>>>>>>>>> BIBLE VERSE <<<<<<<<<
MAPPING

-Define the underlined words.

The heavens <u>declare</u> the glory of God;
the skies <u>proclaim</u> the work of his hands. Day after day
they pour forth speech; night after night they reveal
knowledge.

★ _____
_____
_____
_____

★ _____
_____
_____
_____

 DAILY TASKS

☐ Bible verse penmanship practice

☐ Practice your spelling words

☐ Individual reading time for 15-20 minutes

☐ Complete worksheets in your workbook

☐ History/Geography

MY DAY

Please fill in this information about your day.

DATE: ___/___/___

WEATHER

TIME: _____

Please practice writing this part of our memory verse.

"Blessed are the merciful,
for they will be shown mercy."

Matthew 5:7

COUNTRY STUDY

Have your parent help you get these answers from books or the internet.

Country to study:

_____

_____

Draw a photo of the countries flag
in the box provided.

1. What is the population?

_____

2. What is the climate?

_____

3. What are the 3 largest cities?

_____

_____

_____

4. Are people able to be Christians without persecution?

_____

5. What is the primary source of income?

_____

6. How is their government structured?

_____

7. What is the main people group? What is the main language spoken?

_____

DAILY TASKS

☐ Bible verse penmanship practice

☐ Practice your spelling words

☐ Individual reading time for 15-20 minutes

☐ Complete worksheets in your workbook

☐ Science

JOURNALING MY WEEK

Please write 1-2 sentences about your week. You may choose to tell something you have learned, done, or experienced.

_____

_____

_____

_____

_____

_____

_____

_____

Please draw a picture of something I read about from the Bible.

Please practice writing this part of our memory verse.

"Blessed are the merciful,
for they will be shown mercy."

Matthew 5:7

SPELLING
PRACTICE

Please write each of your spelling words two times.

_____   _____

_____   _____

_____   _____

_____   _____

_____   _____

_____   _____

_____   _____

WRITE A LETTER

*Parents: Help your child write a properly formatted letter including a greeting, body, closing, and signature. (If you struggle to remember this look up "personal letter format". Don't forget to add any misspelled words to your child's spelling list. Explain placement of the address, return address, and stamp. Tell your child the price of a stamp.

Please write a letter to a friend or family member. Have your parent edit your letter. Correct any mistakes in spelling or grammar.

Address the envelope for your letter and put your return address with the help of your parent. Each time you send a letter you will get more confident in this. Use good penmanship so the post office can easily read what you wrote.

DAILY TASKS

☐ Bible verse penmanship practice

☐ Spelling test

☐ Individual reading time for 15-20 minutes

☐ Complete worksheets in your workbook

☐ Check your work for the week, review anything that felt challenging

FACT OF THE WEEK

TYPES OF HABITATS

There are various types of habitats on our planet. Each habitat has distinctive characteristics that provide a unique home for a diverse array of plants and animals.

Ocean

Desert

Wetland

Polar Region

Forest

Grassland

Mountain

STORIES FROM SCRIPTURE
WRITING PROJECT

Please choose one of the stories we have read from the Bible this week to write about. Imagine you are telling the story to someone who has never heard it. Tell them why you like this story and what it means to you. Answer the 5 W questions to help you write. Use additional notebook paper if needed.

Who? _____

What? _____

When? _____

Where? _____

Why? _____

_____

_____

_____

_____

_____

_____

_____

_____

_____

DAILY TASKS

☐ Bible verse penmanship practice

☐ Practice your spelling words

☐ Individual reading time for 15-20 minutes

☐ Complete worksheets in your workbook

☐ Work on your unit art project or handicraft

BIBLE JOURNALING

Please write one sentence about something you learned that was meaningful to you from our Bible time today.

_____

_____

_____

_____

_____

_____

_____

_____

Please draw a picture of something I read about from the Bible.

Please practice writing this part of our memory verse.

"Blessed are the peacemakers,
for they will be called children of God."

Matthew 5:9

DAILY TASKS

☐ Bible verse penmanship practice

☐ Practice your spelling words

☐ Individual reading time for 15-20 minutes

☐ Complete worksheets in your workbook

☐ History/Geography

MY DAY

Please fill in this information about your day.

DATE: _____ / _____ / _____

WEATHER

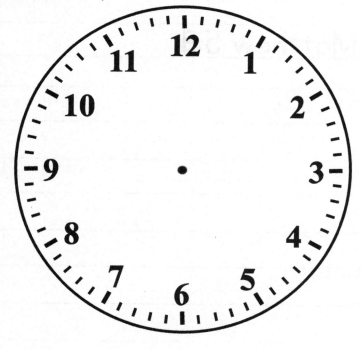

TIME: _____

Please practice writing this part of our memory verse.

"Blessed are the peacemakers,
for they will be called children of God."

Matthew 5:9

COUNTRY STUDY

We are going to use the information you gathered last week to choose a project to do on the country you chose to study. You have options to choose from. Please work with your parent to choose one that will work best for you.

1. Make a photo collage/information poster like we did for our continent study. Remember to include valuable information. Present this to your family or friends and share with them interesting facts you learned about this country.

2. Make a traditional food from the country you are studying. You will need help from your parents with this. Serve the food to your family and share about the country it originates from.

3. Write a report about Christians in the country you chose. Include details about missions, persecution, laws, and family pressure. Include names of prominent missionaries or evangelists. Include the history of Christianity and the current state of the Church.

Project choice
_____
_____

What is needed for your project?
_____
_____
_____

Have fun and do your best!

_____

Please write the name of the country you have chosen.

Draw a picture of the country.

Please write some interesting facts your learn about this country. Include some details about how they live and what they eat.

_____

_____

_____

_____

_____

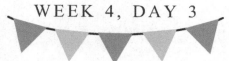

DAILY TASKS

☐ Bible verse penmanship practice

☐ Practice your spelling words

☐ Individual reading time for 15-20 minutes

☐ Complete worksheets in your workbook

☐ Science

BOOK SUMMARY

Please write a short summary of a book you have been reading for your individual reading time.

TITLE: _____

AUTHOR: _____

_____

_____

_____

_____

_____

Please draw a picture of something I read about from the Bible.

Please practice writing this part of our memory verse.

"Blessed are the peacemakers,
for they will be called children of God."

Matthew 5:9

SPELLING
PRACTICE

Please write each of your spelling words two times.

_____   _____

_____   _____

_____   _____

_____   _____

_____   _____

_____   _____

_____   _____

Please write two sentences using at least three of your spelling words.

_____

_____

_____

_____

_____

224

SOLAR SYSTEM
SCIENCE WORKSHEET

Please label the planets.

_____

_____

_____

_____

_____

_____

_____

_____

DAILY TASKS

☐ Bible verse penmanship practice

☐ Spelling test

☐ Individual reading time for 15-20 minutes

☐ Complete worksheets in your workbook

☐ Check your work for the week, review anything that felt challenging

FACT OF THE WEEK

Please read this information. It is fun to learn new things!

ANIMAL FACTS

Zebras are related to horses. They eat mainly grass, shrubs, leaves, and bark. No two zebras have the same stripe pattern!

ZEBRA

HISTORICAL

PERSON OF INTEREST

Please choose a person you have learned about to answer these questions and write a report. You may need your parent to help you locate these facts using the internet or the book you have been reading. On the back, please write two to three paragraphs about this person.

1. Who are you learning about?

_____

_____

2. What did they do?

_____

_____

3. When did they live?

_____

_____

4. Where did they live?

_____

_____

5. Why would someone be interested in learning about this person?

_____

_____

_____

_____

_____

_____

_____

Write one paragraph about the person you have chosen. Be sure to include their name, why they are interesting, where they lived, and when they lived there. Imagine you are writing to someone who knows nothing about the person you are writing about.

<u>Paragraph Check List</u>

☐ Topic sentence

☐ Supporting sentences

☐ Closing sentence

☐ The 5 Ws

_____

_____

_____

_____

_____

_____

_____

_____

_____

_____

_____

_____

_____

_____

_____

_____

CREATE YOUR OWN MINI UNIT STUDY

This week you will create a mini-unit study on something you wish to study. Work with your parent to come up with ideas and a plan.

Topic of Study: _____

List of ways to learn about this topic:

_____

_____

_____

_____

_____

_____

Scriptures that apply:

_____

_____

_____

_____

Field trip or activity ideas:

_____

_____

_____

_____

CREATE YOUR OWN MINI UNIT STUDY

Draw a picture of your topic of choice:

UNIT

Five

SPELLING LISTS

Your student's spelling words will come from words you identify that they spell incorrectly in their writing. As your student writes for assignments (or any other writing) please write the words they spell incorrectly here. At the end of the week there will be a spelling quiz. If your student continues to struggle with a word add it to the following week's list.

Week 1	Week 2	Week 3	Week 4

DAILY TASKS

☐ Bible verse penmanship practice

☐ Practice your spelling words (does not begin until week 2)

☐ Individual reading time for 15-20 minutes

☐ Complete worksheets in your workbook

☐ Work on your unit art project or handicraft

BIBLE JOURNALING

Please write one sentence about something you learned that was meaningful to you from our Bible time today.

_____

_____

_____

_____

_____

_____

_____

_____

_____

Please draw a picture of something I read about from the Bible.

Please practice writing this part of our memory verse.

"The Lord is my shepherd, I lack nothing. He makes me lie down in green pastures."

Psalm 23:1a

Tense: past, present, future

We are going to practice making these verbs into past tense. Please write the verb as if you were going to say this action happened yesterday.

run _____

_____

walk _____

_____

jump _____

_____

fly _____

_____

sit _____

_____

make _____

_____

eat _____

_____

DAILY TASKS

☐ Bible verse penmanship practice

☐ Practice your spelling words (does not begin until week 2)

☐ Individual reading time for 15-20 minutes

☐ Complete worksheets in your workbook

☐ History/Geography

MY DAY

Please fill in this information about your day.

DATE: ___/___/___

WEATHER

TIME: _____

Please practice writing this part of our memory verse.

"The Lord is my shepherd, I lack nothing. He makes me lie down in green pastures."

Psalm 23:1a

GRAMMAR
PRACTICE

Please add the given prefix to these words given to create a new word.

<u>Re</u>

new: _____

lease: _____

visit: _____

<u>In</u>

to: _____

side: _____

line: _____

<u>Un</u>

afraid: _____

affected: _____

affordable: _____

CONTINENT STUDY
EUROPE

Work with your parent to get these answers from books or the internet.

1. Where is this continent located? What hemisphere(s) is it in?

_____

_____

2. What is the climate?

_____

_____

3. What oceans are near this continent?

_____

_____

4. How many countries are on this continent?

_____

_____

5. What is the population?

_____

_____

6. How large is this continent?

_____

_____

7. What are the top natural resources?

_____

_____

8. What are the main religions?

_____

_____

- Please label the 3 largest cities, use a red dot to mark.

- Draw in any major rivers or lakes with blue colored pencil

- If the equator crosses this continent please draw a black line to show where.

- Please label the oceans around this continent.

Name of this continent:

_____

_____

We will study one country from this continent. Please choose which country you would like to study and find resources to learn more about this country.

Country:

_____

_____

DAILY TASKS

☐ Bible verse penmanship practice

☐ Practice your spelling words (does not begin until week 2)

☐ Individual reading time for 15-20 minutes

☐ Complete worksheets in your workbook

☐ Science

JOURNALING MY WEEK

Please write 1-2 sentences about your week. You may choose to tell something you have learned, done, or experienced.

_____

_____

_____

_____

_____

_____

_____

_____

_____

Please practice writing this part of our memory verse.

"The Lord is my shepherd, I lack nothing. He makes me lie down in green pastures."

Psalm 23:1a

FISH
SCIENCE WORKSHEET

Please fill in the blank with the correct word from the word bank.

Word Bank

Eggs

Scales

Cold

Carnivores

Gills

1. Fish are _____ blooded

2. Fish reproduce by laying _____

3. Most fish are _____

4. Fish breathe through their _____

5. Most fish have _____

List one species of fish that lives in each of these locations. Remember: rivers, lakes, and ponds are fresh water while the ocean is salt water.

_____   _____

SPELLING
PRACTICE

Please write each of your spelling words two times.

_____   _____

_____   _____

_____   _____

_____   _____

_____   _____

_____   _____

_____   _____

Please write two sentences using at least three of your spelling words.

_____

_____

_____

_____

_____

DAILY TASKS

☐ Bible verse penmanship practice

☐ Spelling test (not until week 2)

☐ Individual reading time for 15-20 minutes

☐ Complete worksheets in your workbook

☐ Check your work for the week, review anything that felt challenging

FACT OF THE WEEK

Please read this information. It is fun to learn new things!

ANIMAL FACTS

ELEPHANT

African Elephants have an amazing memory. Their diet consists of grass, fruit, leaves, twigs, and bark. Their ears can grow up to 5 feet long!

STORIES FROM SCRIPTURE
WRITING PROJECT

Please choose one of the stories we have read from the Bible this week to write about. Imagine you are telling the story to someone who has never heard it. Tell them why you like this story and what it means to you. Answer the 5 W questions to help you write. Use additional notebook paper if needed.

Who? _____

What? _____

When? _____

Where? _____

Why? _____

_____

_____

_____

_____

_____

_____

_____

DAILY TASKS

- ☐ Bible verse penmanship practice

- ☐ Practice your spelling words

- ☐ Individual reading time for 15-20 minutes

- ☐ Complete worksheets in your workbook

- ☐ Work on your unit art project or handicraft

BIBLE JOURNALING

Please write one sentence about something you learned that was meaningful to you from our Bible time today.

_____

_____

_____

_____

_____

_____

_____

_____

Please practice writing this part of our memory verse.

"Even though I walk through the darkest valley,
I will fear no evil, for you are with me; your
rod and your staff, they comfort me."

Psalm 23:4

GRAMMAR
PRACTICE

Please write one example of each of these parts of speech.

Noun:

_____

_____

Pronoun:

_____

_____

Verb:

_____

_____

Adjective:

_____

_____

Please write the following sentences. If you need help, ask your parent.

Please write a sentence using the past tense of the word <u>run</u>.

_____

_____

Please write a sentence using the plural of <u>child.</u>

_____

_____

DAILY TASKS

☐ Bible verse penmanship practice

☐ Practice your spelling words

☐ Individual reading time for 15-20 minutes

☐ Complete worksheets in your workbook

☐ History/Geography

MY DAY

Please fill in this information about your day.

DATE: _____ / ___ / _____

WEATHER

TIME: _____

Please draw a picture of something I read about from the Bible.

Please practice writing this part of our memory verse.

"Even though I walk through the darkest valley, I will fear no evil, for you are with me; your rod and your staff, they comfort me."

Psalm 23:4

BIBLE VERSE

GRAMMAR PRACTICE

Please read Psalm 23, our unit verse. Look up the underlined words using a dictionary and read the definition. Choose <u>two</u> words to record the definition on the lines provided.

"The Lord is my shepherd, I lack nothing. He makes me lie down in green <u>pastures</u>, he leads me beside quiet waters, he <u>refreshes</u> my soul. He guides me along the right paths for his name's sake. Even though I walk through the darkest valley, I will fear no evil,

for you are with me; your rod and your staff, they <u>comfort</u> me.

You prepare a table before me in the presence of my enemies.

You <u>anoint</u> my head with oil; my cup overflows.

Surely your goodness and love will follow me all the days of my life, and I will <u>dwell</u> in the house of the Lord forever."

Psalm 23

_____

_____

_____

_____

_____

_____

_____

_____

_____

_____

CONTINENT STUDY
EUROPE

Today you are going to take the information you learned last week and make it into a poster report. Please include a picture of the continent, details about the population, size, and climate. Share your report with your family or friends and tell them about the continent you studied.

Population:

Size:

Climate:

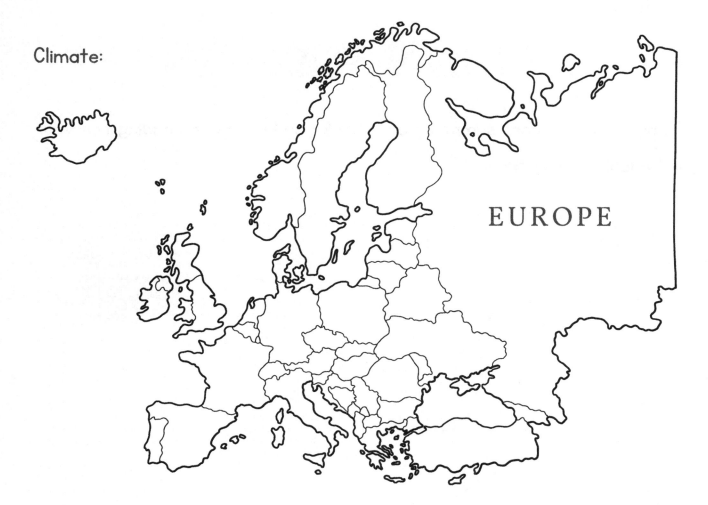

DAILY TASKS

☐ Bible verse penmanship practice

☐ Practice your spelling words

☐ Individual reading time for 15-20 minutes

☐ Complete worksheets in your workbook

☐ Science

BOOK SUMMARY

Please write a short summary of a book you have been reading for your individual reading time.

TITLE: _____

AUTHOR: _____

_____

_____

_____

_____

_____

Please practice writing this part of our memory verse.

"Even though I walk through the darkest valley, I will fear no evil, for you are with me; your rod and your staff, they comfort me."

Psalm 23:4

SPELLING
PRACTICE

Please write each of your spelling words two times.

_____   _____

_____   _____

_____   _____

_____   _____

_____   _____

_____   _____

_____   _____

_____   _____

Please write two sentences using at least three of your spelling words.

_____

_____

_____

_____

_____

SPECIES- FISH
SCIENCE WORKSHEET

Please choose one species of fish to answer these questions about.

SPECIES

SCIENTIFIC NAME

MY HABITAT

DRAW A PICTURE

DETAILS ABOUT ME

What I eat, how I look, anything that makes me unique

DAILY TASKS

- ☐ Bible verse penmanship practice

- ☐ Spelling test

- ☐ Individual reading time for 15-20 minutes

- ☐ Complete worksheets in your workbook

- ☐ Check your work for the week, review anything that felt challenging

FACT OF THE WEEK

Please read this information. It is fun to learn new things!

ANIMAL FACTS

Tigers can weigh up to 450lbs. Tigers are meat eaters and prefer to do their hunting alone. Their teeth can be up to four inches long!

TIGER

EDITING
PRACTICE

Please look at the following story and correct any mistakes in capitalization and punctuation. Remember, days of the week, months, and proper nouns are all capitalized.

sam and steve want to go fishing with their dad. mom is going blueberry picking. Siter lucy has to decide between fishing and berry picking. she loves to spend time with Sam and steve, but she really likes picking berries Mom promises that lucy can help make a blueberry pie to take to fellowship on friday if she comes berry picking. Lucy cannot turn that offer down! she promises Sam and steve that she will have a bowl of berries for each of them

HISTORICAL

PERSON OF INTEREST

Please choose a person you have learned about to answer these questions and write a report. You may need your parent to help you locate these facts using the internet or the book you have been reading. On the back please write one paragraph about this person.

1. Who are you learning about?

_____

_____

2. What did they do?

_____

_____

3. When did they live?

_____

_____

4. Where did they live?

_____

_____

5. Why would someone be interested in learning about this person?

_____

_____

_____

_____

_____

Write one paragraph about the person you have chosen. Be sure to include their name, why they are interesting, where they lived, and when they lived there. Imagine you are writing to someone who knows nothing about the person you are writing about.

<u>Paragraph Check List</u>

☐ Topic sentence

☐ Supporting sentences

☐ Closing sentence

☐ The 5 Ws

_____

_____

_____

_____

_____

_____

_____

_____

_____

_____

_____

_____

_____

DAILY TASKS

☐ Bible verse penmanship practice

☐ Practice your spelling words

☐ Individual reading time for 15-20 minutes

☐ Complete worksheets in your workbook

☐ Work on your unit art project or handicraft

BIBLE JOURNALING

Please write one sentence about something you learned that was meaningful to you from our Bible time today.

_____

_____

_____

_____

_____

_____

_____

_____

_____

Please draw a picture of something I read about from the Bible.

Please practice writing this part of our memory verse.

"You prepare a table before me in the presence of my enemies."

Psalm 23:5a

<u>Punctuation Practice-</u> Please add commas in the following lists. Please add commas to the dates and write them in short form.

List example:

We are going to bake cookies, bread, and cake today.

Date examples:

Sunday, May 18, 2022   5-18-22

Mom brought pillows blankets and coats for our camping trip.

I enjoy eating zucchini lettuce carrots peas and potatoes from our garden.

We work on school Monday Tuesday Wednesday and Thursday.

I have visited Hawaii Michigan Washington and California

Saturday December 15 2021 _____

Monday June 3, 2022 _____

Thursday July 4, 2023 _____

DAILY TASKS

☐ Bible verse penmanship practice

☐ Practice your spelling words

☐ Individual reading time for 15-20 minutes

☐ Complete worksheets in your workbook

☐ History/Geography

MY DAY

Please fill in this information about your day.

DATE: _____ / _____ / _____

WEATHER

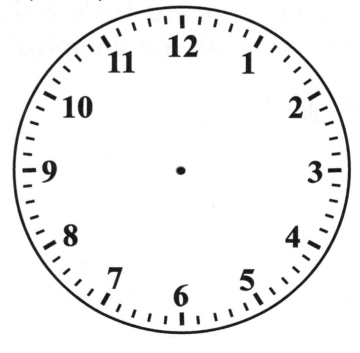

TIME: _____

Please practice writing this part of our memory verse.

"You prepare a table before me in the
presence of my enemies."

Psalm 23:5a

COUNTRY STUDY

Have your parent help you get these answers from books or the internet.

Country to study:
_____

_____

Draw a photo of the country's flag
in the box provided.

1. What is the population?
_____

_____

2. What is the climate?
_____

_____

3. What are the 3 largest cities?
_____

_____

_____

4. Are people able to be Christians without persecution?
_____

_____

5. What is the primary source of income?
_____

_____

6. How is their government structured?
_____

_____

7. What is the main people group? What is the main language spoken?
_____

_____

DAILY TASKS

☐ Bible verse penmanship practice

☐ Practice your spelling words

☐ Individual reading time for 15-20 minutes

☐ Complete worksheets in your workbook

☐ Science

JOURNALING MY WEEK

Please write 1-2 sentences about your week. You may choose to tell something you have learned, done, or experienced.

_____

_____

_____

_____

_____

_____

_____

_____

Please draw a picture of something I read about from the Bible.

Please practice writing this part of our memory verse.

"You prepare a table before me in the presence of my enemies."

Psalm 23:5a

SPELLING
PRACTICE

Please write each of your spelling words two times.

_____   _____

_____   _____

_____   _____

_____   _____

_____   _____

_____   _____

_____   _____

WRITE A LETTER

*Parents: Help your child write a properly formatted letter including a greeting, body, closing, and signature. (If you struggle to remember this look up "personal letter format". Don't forget to add any misspelled words to your child's spelling list. Explain placement of the address, return address, and stamp. Tell your child the price of a stamp.

Please write a letter to a friend or family member. Have your parent edit your letter. Correct any mistakes in spelling or grammar.

Address the envelope for your letter and put your return address with the help of your parent. Each time you send a letter you will get more confident in this. Use good penmanship so the post office can easily read what you wrote.

LOCAL BIRDS
SCIENCE WORKSHEET

Please look up three species of birds in your area and list them here.
Answer the following questions about each by circling the correct
answer.

Species 1 _____

Do they Migrate?   yes   no

This bird lives mostly on   Water Land

Species 2 _____

Do they Migrate? yes no

This bird lives mostly on Water Land

Species 3 _____

Do they Migrate? yes no

This bird lives mostly on Water Land

DAILY TASKS

☐ Bible verse penmanship practice

☐ Spelling test

☐ Individual reading time for 15-20 minutes

☐ Complete worksheets in your workbook

☐ Check your work for the week, review anything that felt challenging

FACT OF THE WEEK

Please read this information. It is fun to learn new things!

ANIMAL FACTS

Monkeys are known for their playful behavior. They eat many things, but especially seeds, flowers, fruits, and leaves. Monkeys become adults after 3-4 years of life!

MONKEY

# REVIEW

Please use the following words properly in a sentence.

Their
_____
_____
_____

There
_____
_____
_____

Two
_____
_____
_____

To
_____
_____
_____

Too
_____
_____

STORIES FROM SCRIPTURE
WRITING PROJECT

Please choose one of the stories we have read from the Bible this week to write about. Imagine you are telling the story to someone who has never heard it. Tell them why you like this story and what it means to you. Answer the 5 W questions to help you write. Use additional notebook paper if needed.

Who? _____

What? _____

When? _____

Where? _____

Why? _____

_____

_____

_____

_____

_____

_____

_____

 DAILY TASKS

☐ Bible verse penmanship practice

☐ Practice your spelling words

☐ Individual reading time for 15-20 minutes

☐ Complete worksheets in your workbook

☐ Work on your unit art project or handicraft

BIBLE JOURNALING

Please write one sentence about something you learned that was meaningful to you from our Bible time today.

_____

_____

_____

_____

_____

_____

_____

_____

Please draw a picture of something I read about from the Bible.

Please practice writing this part of our memory verse.

"Surely your goodness and love will follow me all the days of my life, and I will dwell in the house of the Lord forever.

Psalm 23:6

<u>Contractions:</u>

Please write the following words as contractions.

I am _____

They are _____

We are _____

He is _____

She is _____

You will _____

They will _____

They did _____

She did _____

He did _____

DAILY TASKS

☐ Bible verse penmanship practice

☐ Practice your spelling words

☐ Individual reading time for 15-20 minutes

☐ Complete worksheets in your workbook

☐ History/Geography

MY DAY

Please fill in this information about your day.

DATE: ___ / ___ / ___

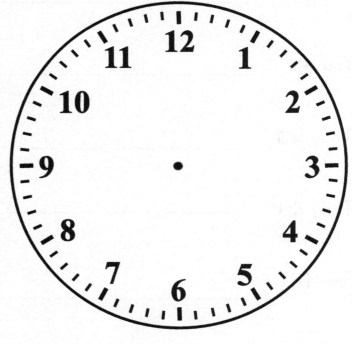

WEATHER

TIME: _____

Please practice writing this part of our memory verse.

"Surely your goodness and love will follow me all the days of my life, and I will dwell in the house of the Lord forever.

Psalm 23:6

COUNTRY STUDY

We are going to use the information you gathered last week to choose a project to do on the country you chose to study. You have options to choose from. Please work with your parent to choose one that will work best for you.

1. Make a photo collage/information poster like we did for our continent study. Remember to include valuable information. Present this to your family or friends and share with them interesting facts you learned about this country.

2. Make a traditional food from the country you are studying. You will need help from your parents with this. Serve the food to your family and share about the country it originates from.

3. Write a report about Christians in the country you chose. Include details about missions, persecution, laws, and family pressure. Include names of prominent missionaries or evangelists. Include the history of Christianity and the current state of the Church.

Project choice
_____

_____

What is needed for your project?
_____

_____

_____

Have fun and do your best!

_____

Please write the name of the country you have chosen.

Draw a picture of the country.

Please write some interesting facts your learn about this country. Include some details about how they live and what they eat.

_____

_____

_____

_____

_____

_____

DAILY TASKS

☐ Bible verse penmanship practice

☐ Practice your spelling words

☐ Individual reading time for 15-20 minutes

☐ Complete worksheets in your workbook

☐ Science

BOOK SUMMARY

Please write a short summary of a book you have been reading for your individual reading time.

TITLE: _____

AUTHOR: _____

_____

_____

_____

_____

_____

Please draw a picture of something I read about from the Bible.

Please practice writing this part of our memory verse.

"Surely your goodness and love will follow me all the days of my life, and I will dwell in the house of the Lord forever.

Psalm 23:6

SPELLING
PRACTICE

Please write each of your spelling words two times.

_____   _____

_____   _____

_____   _____

_____   _____

_____   _____

_____   _____

_____   _____

Please write two sentences using at least three of your spelling words.

_____

_____

_____

_____

_____

SPECIES- BIRDS
SCIENCE WORKSHEET

Please choose one species to answer these questions about.

SPECIES

SCIENTIFIC NAME

MY HABITAT

DRAW A PICTURE

DETAILS ABOUT ME

What I eat, how I look, anything that makes me unique

DAILY TASKS

☐ Bible verse penmanship practice

☐ Spelling test

☐ Individual reading time for 15-20 minutes

☐ Complete worksheets in your workbook

☐ Check your work for the week, review anything that felt challenging

FACT OF THE WEEK

Please read this information. It is fun to learn new things!

ANIMAL FACTS

Pandas will eat small animals and fish, but 99% of their diet is made up of bamboo. Unlike most other bears, panda bears do not hibernate!

PANDA

BIBLE VERSE

MAPPING

-Define the underlined words.

"When she and the members of her household were baptized, she invited us to her home. "If you <u>consider</u> me a believer in the Lord," she said, "come and stay at my house." And she <u>persuaded</u> us."

Acts 16:15

★ _____

_____

_____

_____

★ _____

_____

_____

_____

HISTORICAL

PERSON OF INTEREST

Please choose a person you have learned about to answer these questions and write a report. You may need your parent to help you locate these facts using the internet or the book you have been reading. On the back please write one paragraph about this person.

1. Who are you learning about?

_____

_____

2. What did they do?

_____

_____

3. When did they live?

_____

_____

4. Where did they live?

_____

_____

5. Why would someone be interested in learning about this person?

_____

_____

_____

_____

_____

_____

_____

Write one paragraph about the person you have chosen. Be sure to include their name, why they are interesting, where they lived, and when they lived there. Imagine you are writing to someone who knows nothing about the person you are writing about.

Paragraph Check List

☐ Topic sentence

☐ Supporting sentences

☐ Closing sentence

☐ The 5 Ws

_____

_____

_____

_____

_____

_____

_____

_____

_____

_____

_____

_____

_____

_____

CREATE YOUR OWN MINI UNIT STUDY

This week you will create a mini-unit study on something you wish to study. Work with your parent to come up with ideas and a plan.

Topic of Study: _____

List of ways to learn about this topic:
_____
_____
_____
_____
_____
_____

Scriptures that apply:
_____
_____
_____
_____

Field trip or activity ideas:
_____
_____
_____
_____

CREATE YOUR OWN MINI UNIT STUDY

Draw a picture of your topic of choice:

UNIT
Six

UNIT
Six

SPELLING LISTS

Your student's spelling words will come from words you identify that they spell incorrectly in their writing. As your student writes for assignments (or any other writing) please write the words they spell incorrectly here. At the end of the week there will be a spelling quiz. If your student continues to struggle with a word add it to the following week's list.

Week 1	Week 2	Week 3	Week 4

DAILY TASKS

☐ Bible verse penmanship practice

☐ Practice your spelling words

☐ Individual reading time for 15-20 minutes

☐ Complete worksheets in your workbook

☐ Work on your unit art project or handicraft

BIBLE JOURNALING

Please write one sentence about something you learned that was meaningful to you from our Bible time today.

_____

_____

_____

_____

_____

_____

_____

_____

_____

Please draw a picture of something I read about from the Bible.

Please practice writing this part of our memory verse.

"The God who made the world and everything in it is the Lord of heaven and earth and does not live in temples built by human hands."

Acts 17:24a

Please underline the nouns, circle the verbs, and box the adjectives in the following sentences.

God created the bright sunshine.

Jesus walked along the deep Sea of Galilee.

James helps his elderly mother sit down.

State of Being Verbs: a word that doesn't show action but shows a state of being, is considered a verb.

am	be
is	being
are	been
was	
were	

Please write a sentence using a state of being verb.

_____

_____

_____

WEEK 1, DAY 2

DAILY TASKS

☐ Bible verse penmanship practice

☐ Practice your spelling words

☐ Individual reading time for 15-20 minutes

☐ Complete worksheets in your workbook

☐ History/Geography

MY DAY

Please fill in this information about your day.

DATE: _____ / _____ / _____

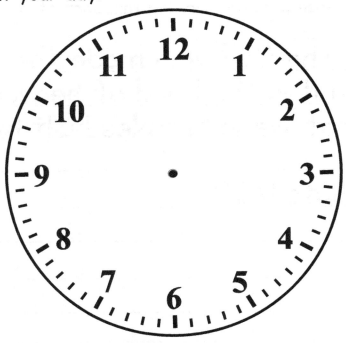

WEATHER

TIME: _____

Please practice writing this part of our memory verse.

"The God who made the world and everything in it is the Lord of heaven and earth and does not live in temples built by human hands."

Acts 17:24a

GRAMMAR
PRACTICE

Please change the tense of these verbs to fit in the sentences. Please ask your parent for help if these are difficult.

I *play*_____ with my friends yesterday.

Jesus *multiply*_____ bread and fish.

I like to *ate*_____ cake on my birthday.

I am *running*_____ after my puppy when he gets

away.

Please fill in a verb that fits the proper tense for these sentences.

I _____ my horse to the mountain.

I am_____ to my grandma's house.

Tom_____ me my ball back yesterday.

CONTINENT STUDY
NORTH AMERICA

Work with your parent to get these answers from books or the internet.

1. Where is this continent located? What hemisphere(s) is it in?

_____

_____

2. What is the climate?

_____

_____

3. What oceans are near this continent?

_____

_____

4. How many countries are on this continent?

_____

_____

5. What is the population?

_____

_____

6. How large is this continent?

_____

_____

7. What are the top natural resources?

_____

_____

8. What are the main religions?

_____

_____

- Please label the 3 largest cities, use a red dot to mark.

- Draw in any major rivers or lakes with blue colored pencil

- If the equator crosses this continent please draw a black line to show where.

- Please label the oceans around this continent.

Name of this continent:

_____

_____

We will study one country from this continent. Please choose which country you would like to study and find resources to learn more about this country.

Country:

_____

_____

CONTINENT STUDY
SOUTH AMERICA

Work with your parent to get these answers from books or the internet.

1. Where is this continent located? What hemisphere(s) is it in?

_____

_____

2. What is the climate?

_____

_____

3. What oceans are near this continent?

_____

_____

4. How many countries are on this continent?

_____

_____

5. What is the population?

_____

_____

6. How large is this continent?

_____

_____

7. What are the top natural resources?

_____

_____

8. What are the main religions?

_____

_____

- Please label the
  3 largest cities,
  use a red dot
  to mark.
- Draw in any major rivers
  or lakes with blue colored
  pencil
- If the equator crosses
  this continent please
  draw a black line to show
  where.
- Please label the oceans
  around this continent.

Name of this continent:

_____

_____

We will study one country

from this continent. Please choose

which country you would like to study

and find resources to learn more about

this country.

Country:

_____

_____

DAILY TASKS

☐ Bible verse penmanship practice

☐ Practice your spelling words

☐ Individual reading time for 15-20 minutes

☐ Complete worksheets in your workbook

☐ Science 💡

JOURNALING MY WEEK

Please write 1-2 sentences about your week. You may choose to tell something you have learned, done, or experienced.

_____

_____

_____

_____

_____

_____

_____

_____

_____

Please practice writing this part of our memory verse.

"The God who made the world and everything in it is the Lord of heaven and earth and does not live in temples built by human hands."

Acts 17:24a

SPELLING
PRACTICE

Please write each of your spelling words two times.

_____   _____

_____   _____

_____   _____

_____   _____

_____   _____

_____   _____

_____   _____

Please write two sentences using at least three of your spelling words.

_____

_____

_____

_____

_____

DAILY TASKS

☐ Bible verse penmanship practice

☐ Spelling test

☐ Individual reading time for 15-20 minutes

☐ Complete worksheets in your workbook

☐ Check your work for the week, review anything that felt challenging

FACT OF THE WEEK

Please read this information. It is fun to learn new things!

Plants can live in jungles, deserts, and almost everywhere else you can think of. Let's explore some examples of plants, their habitats, and how they survive.

Aloe Plants

- They grow well in dry, arid places.
- Their **fleshy stems, leaves, and roots** allow them to store much water.
- The **thick waxy coating** on their leaves helps prevent excessive moisture loss.

STORIES FROM SCRIPTURE
WRITING PROJECT

Please choose one of the stories we have read from the Bible this week to write about. Imagine you are telling the story to someone who has never heard it. Tell them why you like this story and what it means to you. Answer the 5 W questions to help you write at least one paragraph. Use notebook paper to write, or type your paper on the computer. When you are finished writing, edit your work. Check for complete sentences, proper capitalization, and punctuation. Have your parent offer suggestions for ways to improve your writing. Be sure they edit for spelling. Add any words that are incorrect to next week's spelling list.

Who?_____

What? _____

When? _____

Where?_____

Why? _____

DAILY TASKS

☐ Bible verse penmanship practice

☐ Practice your spelling words

☐ Individual reading time for 15-20 minutes

☐ Complete worksheets in your workbook

☐ Work on your unit art project or handicraft

BIBLE JOURNALING

Please write one sentence about something you learned that was meaningful to you from our Bible time today.

_____

_____

_____

_____

_____

_____

_____

_____

Please practice writing this part of our memory verse.

"He himself gives everyone life and breath and
everything else."
Acts 17:25b

GRAMMAR
PRACTICE

Please put an S next to the nouns that are singular and a P next to the nouns that are plural.

horse ☐

cows ☐

geese ☐

people ☐

man ☐

women ☐

child ☐

Please write a sentence using a plural noun.

_____

_____

Please write a sentence using a singular noun.

_____

_____

DAILY TASKS

☐ Bible verse penmanship practice

☐ Practice your spelling words

☐ Individual reading time for 15-20 minutes

☐ Complete worksheets in your workbook

☐ History/Geography

MY DAY

Please fill in this information about your day.

DATE: _____ / _____ / _____

WEATHER

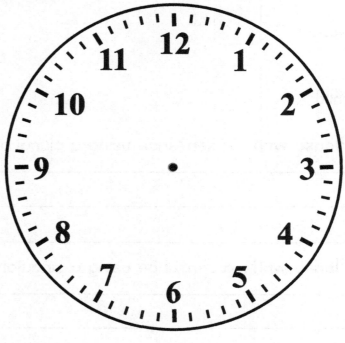

TIME: _____

Please draw a picture of something I read about from the Bible.

Please practice writing this part of our memory verse.

"He himself gives everyone life and breath and everything else."
Acts 17:25b

CONTINENT STUDY

NORTH AMERICA

Today you are going to take the information you learned last week and make it into a poster report. Please include a picture of the continent, details about the population, size, and climate. Share your report with your family or friends and tell them about the continent you studied.

Population:

Size:

Climate:

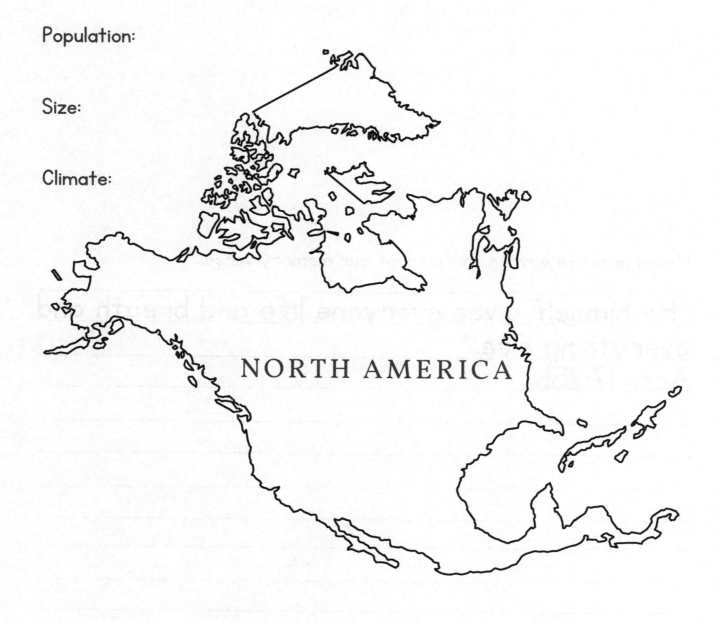

NORTH AMERICA

CONTINENT STUDY
SOUTH AMERICA

Today you are going to take the information you learned last week and make it into a poster report. Please include a picture of the continent, details about the population, size, and climate. Share your report with your family or friends and tell them about the continent you studied.

Population:

Size:

Climate:

SOUTH AMERICA

DAILY TASKS

☐ Bible verse penmanship practice

☐ Practice your spelling words

☐ Individual reading time for 15-20 minutes

☐ Complete worksheets in your workbook

☐ Science

BOOK SUMMARY

Please write a short summary of a book you have been reading for your individual reading time.

TITLE: _____

AUTHOR: _____

_____

_____

_____

_____

_____

Please practice writing this part of our memory verse.

"He himself gives everyone life and breath and everything else."
Acts 17:25b

SPELLING
PRACTICE

Please write each of your spelling words two times.

_____   _____

_____   _____

_____   _____

_____   _____

_____   _____

_____   _____

_____   _____

_____   _____

Please write two sentences using at least three of your spelling words.

_____

_____

_____

_____

_____

SPECIES- ANIMALS
SCIENCE WORKSHEET

Please choose one species of animal to answer these questions about.

SPECIES

SCIENTIFIC NAME

MY HABITAT

DRAW A PICTURE

DETAILS ABOUT ME

What I eat, how I look, anything that makes me unique

DAILY TASKS

☐ Bible verse penmanship practice

☐ Spelling test

☐ Individual reading time for 15-20 minutes

☐ Complete worksheets in your workbook

☐ Check your work for the week, review anything that felt challenging

FACT OF THE WEEK

Please read this information. It is fun to learn new things!

Baobab Trees

- They survive in low-lying, arid regions.
- Their **spongy trunk** allows them to store up to 100,000 liters of water.
- Some varieties have **slick and shiny bark** that reflects light and keep them cool.

EDITING
PRACTICE

Please look at the following story and correct any mistakes in capitalization and punctuation. Remember, days of the week, months, and proper nouns are all capitalized.

my dad reads his Bible every day Sometimes he reads in the morning, sometimes in the evening. i like to read my bible with him. i am learning to read well enough that i read an adult bible now. it is good to read It helps us to learn new things There are many books I enjoy, but the best book of all is the bible. my parents say we must be thankful we have our own bible because some people do not have a bible. i want everyone to have a bible!

HISTORICAL
PERSON OF INTEREST

Please choose a person you have learned about to answer these questions and write a report. You may need your parent to help you locate these facts using the internet or the book you have been reading. On the back please write one paragraph about this person.

1. Who are you learning about?

_____

_____

2. What did they do?

_____

_____

3. When did they live?

_____

_____

4. Where did they live?

_____

_____

5. Why would someone be interested in learning about this person?

_____

_____

_____

_____

_____

Write one paragraph about the person you have chosen. Be sure to include their name, why they are interesting, where they lived, and when they lived there. Imagine you are writing to someone who knows nothing about the person you are writing about.

<u>Paragraph Check List</u>

☐ Topic sentence

☐ Supporting sentences

☐ Closing sentence

☐ The 5 Ws

_____

_____

_____

_____

_____

_____

_____

_____

_____

_____

_____

_____

_____

_____

_____

_____

_____

DAILY TASKS

☐ Bible verse penmanship practice

☐ Practice your spelling words

☐ Individual reading time for 15-20 minutes

☐ Complete worksheets in your workbook

☐ Work on your unit art project or handicraft

BIBLE JOURNALING

Please write one sentence about something you learned that was meaningful to you from our Bible time today.

_____

_____

_____

_____

_____

_____

_____

_____

_____

Please draw a picture of something I read about from the Bible.

Please practice writing this part of our memory verse.

"Therefore since we are God's offspring, we should not think that the divine being is like gold or silver or stone."

Acts 17:29a

<u>a/an practice-</u> We use the word "a" when the word that follows begins with a consonant. We use the word "an" when the word that follows begins with a vowel or vowel sound. Please fill in "a" or "an" with the word that represents each picture.

DAILY TASKS

☐ Bible verse penmanship practice

☐ Practice your spelling words

☐ Individual reading time for 15-20 minutes

☐ Complete worksheets in your workbook

☐ History/Geography

MY DAY

Please fill in this information about your day.

DATE: _____ / _____ / _____

WEATHER

TIME: _____

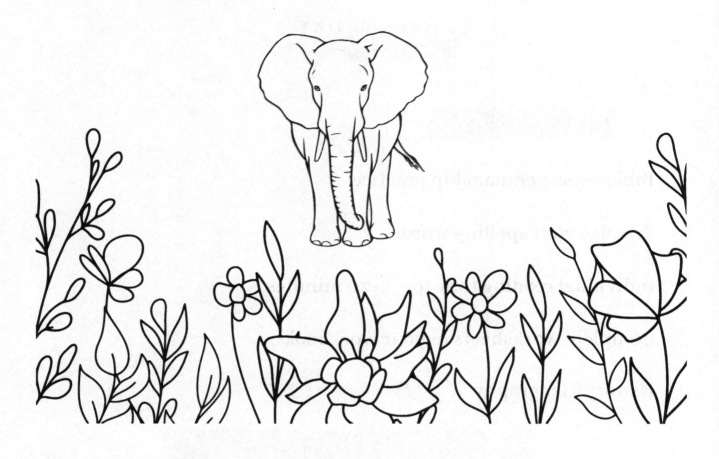

Please practice writing this part of our memory verse.

"Therefore since we are God's offspring, we should not think that the divine being is like gold or silver or stone."

Acts 17:29a

COUNTRY STUDY

Have your parent help you get these answers from books or the internet.

Country to study:

_____

_____

Draw a photo of the country's flag

in the box provided.

1 . What is the population?

_____

2 . What is the climate?

_____

3 . What are the 3 largest cities?

_____

_____

_____

4 . Are people able to be Christians without persecution?

_____

5 . What is the primary source of income?

_____

6 . How is their government structured?

_____

7 . What is the main people group? What is the main language spoken?

_____

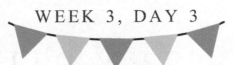

DAILY TASKS

☐ Bible verse penmanship practice

☐ Practice your spelling words

☐ Individual reading time for 15-20 minutes

☐ Complete worksheets in your workbook

☐ Science

JOURNALING MY WEEK

Please write 1-2 sentences about your week. You may choose to tell something you have learned, done, or experienced.

_____

_____

_____

_____

_____

_____

_____

_____

Please draw a picture of something I read about from the Bible.

Please practice writing this part of our memory verse.

"Therefore since we are God's offspring, we should not think that the divine being is like gold or silver or stone."

Acts 17:29a

SPELLING
PRACTICE

Please write each of your spelling words two times.

_____   _____

_____   _____

_____   _____

_____   _____

_____   _____

_____   _____

_____   _____

WRITE A LETTER

*Parents: Help your child write a properly formatted letter including a greeting, body, closing, and signature. (If you struggle to remember this look up "personal letter format". Don't forget to add any misspelled words to your child's spelling list. Explain placement of the address, return address, and stamp. Tell your child the price of a stamp.

Please write a letter to a friend or family member. Have your parent edit your letter. Correct any mistakes in spelling or grammar.

Address the envelope for your letter and put your return address with the help of your parent. Each time you send a letter you will get more confident in this. Use good penmanship so the post office can easily read what you wrote.

ALL ABOUT YOU
SCIENCE WORKSHEET

Please answer these questions about yourself. You can add your fingerprint to the outline of your hand.

YOUR HEIGHT

YOUR WEIGHT

YOUR HAND

DRAW A PICTURE

DETAILS ABOUT YOU

DAILY TASKS

☐ Bible verse penmanship practice

☐ Spelling test

☐ Individual reading time for 15-20 minutes

☐ Complete worksheets in your workbook

☐ Check your work for the week, review anything that felt challenging

FACT OF THE WEEK

Please read this information. It is fun to learn new things!

Conifer Trees

- They can survive the harsh and freezing winters.
- Their long, needle-like leaves have **waxy coatings** that reduce moisture loss.
- They also produce **cones** instead of flowers.

REVEIW

Please match the definition to the word.

pronoun   am, is, are, was, were, be, being, been

adjective   Words that replace a noun

state of being verbs   Words that describe a noun

Please write the abbreviations for the following words.

October   _____

December _____

September_____

January   _____

STORIES FROM SCRIPTURE
WRITING PROJECT

Please choose one of the stories we have read from the Bible this week to write about. Imagine you are telling the story to someone who has never heard it. Tell them why you like this story and what it means to you. Answer the 5 W questions to help you write. Use additional notebook paper if needed.

Who? _____

What? _____

When? _____

Where? _____

Why? _____

_____

_____

_____

_____

_____

_____

_____

_____

WEEK 4, DAY 1

DAILY TASKS

☐ Bible verse penmanship practice

☐ Practice your spelling words

☐ Individual reading time for 15-20 minutes

☐ Complete worksheets in your workbook

☐ Work on your unit art project or handicraft

BIBLE JOURNALING

Please write one sentence about something you learned that was meaningful to you from our Bible time today.

_____

_____

_____

_____

_____

_____

_____

_____

_____

_____

Please draw a picture of something I read about from the Bible.

Please practice writing this part of our memory verse.

"In the past God overlooked such ignorance, but now he commands all people everywhere to repent.

Acts 17:30

<u>Conjunctions</u>:

Conjunctions are words that are used to join words, phrases, or clauses together. Please join the following sentences together using one of these conjunctions that will work in the sentence. Ask your parent for help if needed.

Yet: But	Nor: And not
But: However	Or: Either
And: In addition to	So: Therefore
For: Because	

I like reading my Bible. I like singing praises to God.

_____

_____

I will go on a walk. I will go on a bike ride.

_____

_____

It is raining. The sun is shining.

_____

_____

We want fresh vegetables. We will grow a garden.

_____

_____

I have not finished my school work. I have not finished my chores.

_____

_____

DAILY TASKS

☐ Bible verse penmanship practice

☐ Practice your spelling words

☐ Individual reading time for 15-20 minutes

☐ Complete worksheets in your workbook

☐ History/Geography

MY DAY

Please fill in this information about your day.

DATE: _____ / _____ / _____

WEATHER

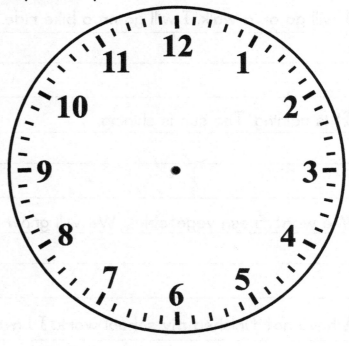

TIME: _____

God made me

Please practice writing this part of our memory verse.

"In the past God overlooked such ignorance, but now he commands all people everywhere to repent.

Acts 17:30

COUNTRY STUDY

We are going to use the information you gathered last week to choose a project to do on the country you chose to study. You have options to choose from. Please work with your parent to choose one that will work best for you.

1. Make a photo collage/information poster like we did for our continent study. Remember to include valuable information. Present this to your family or friends and share with them interesting facts you learned about this country.

2. Make a traditional food from the country you are studying. You will need help from your parents with this. Serve the food to your family and share about the country it originates from.

3. Write a report about Christians in the country you chose. Include details about missions, persecution, laws, and family pressure. Include names of prominent missionaries or evangelists. Include the history of Christianity and the current state of the Church.

Project choice

_____

_____

What is needed for your project?

_____

_____

_____

Have fun and do your best!

_____

Please write the name of the country you have chosen.

Draw a picture of the country.

Please write some interesting facts you have learned about this country.
Include some details about how they live and what they eat.

_____

_____

_____

_____

_____

_____

DAILY TASKS

☐ Bible verse penmanship practice

☐ Practice your spelling words

☐ Individual reading time for 15-20 minutes

☐ Complete worksheets in your workbook

☐ Science 💡

BOOK SUMMARY

Please write a short summary of a book you have been reading for your individual reading time.

TITLE: _____

AUTHOR: _____

_____

_____

_____

_____

_____

Please draw a picture of something I read about from the Bible.

[Drawing box — empty]

Please practice writing this part of our memory verse.

"In the past God overlooked such ignorance, but now he commands all people everywhere to repent.

Acts 17:30

SPELLING
PRACTICE

Please write each of your spelling words two times.

_____   _____

_____   _____

_____   _____

_____   _____

_____   _____

_____   _____

Please write two sentences using at least three of your spelling words.

_____

_____

_____

_____

_____

SYSTEM OF THE HUMAN BODY
SCIENCE WORKSHEET

BODY SYSTEM

ABOUT

DAILY TASKS

☐ Bible verse penmanship practice

☐ Spelling test

☐ Individual reading time for 15-20 minutes

☐ Complete worksheets in your workbook

☐ Check your work for the week, review anything that felt challenging

FACT OF THE WEEK

Please read this information. It is fun to learn new things!

Mangroves

- Mangrove trees sit in swampy, salty, and oxygen-poor environments all year.
- To ensure they get enough oxygen, they **grow roots upward** out of the soil.

<u>Punctuation Practice:</u>

Please add the proper punctuation to the following sentences. Make sure you properly use question marks and exclamation points.

Are you going to visit Israel someday

When I go camping I plan to bring a flashlight my Bible and ingredients to make smores

Ouch That Hurt

Have you read the book of Philippians

What is your favorite memory verse

My mom dad brother and sister are all excited for grandma to visit

Trust in Jesus with all your heart

HISTORICAL
PERSON OF INTEREST

Please choose a person you have learned about to answer these questions and write a report. You may need your parent to help you locate these facts using the internet or the book you have been reading. On the back please write one paragraph about this person.

1. Who are you learning about?

_____

_____

2. What did they do?

_____

_____

3. When did they live?

_____

_____

4. Where did they live?

_____

_____

5. Why would someone be interested in learning about this person?

_____

_____

_____

_____

_____

_____

Write one paragraph about the person you have chosen. Be sure to include their name, why they are interesting, where they lived, and when they lived there. Imagine you are writing to someone who knows nothing about the person you are writing about.

<u>Paragraph Check List</u>

☐ Topic sentence

☐ Supporting sentences

☐ Closing sentence

☐ The 5 Ws

_____

_____

_____

_____

_____

_____

_____

_____

_____

_____

_____

_____

_____

_____

_____

CREATE YOUR OWN MINI UNIT STUDY

This week you will create a mini-unit study on something you wish to study. Work with your parent to come up with ideas and a plan.

Topic of Study: _____

List of ways to learn about this topic:

_____
_____
_____
_____
_____
_____

Scriptures that apply:
_____
_____
_____
_____

Field trip or activity ideas:
_____
_____
_____
_____

CREATE YOUR OWN MINI UNIT STUDY

Draw a picture of your topic of choice:

Handwriting Sheets & Extras

God is with us always.

_____
_____
_____
_____
_____
_____
_____
_____
_____
_____
_____

_____

_____

_____

_____

_____

_____

_____

_____

_____

_____

Wherever
I go,

God goes
with me

Page left blank for double sided printing

Page left blank for double sided printing

Page left blank for double sided printing

Page left blank for double sided printing

Praise God in the storm and in the sun!

Page left blank for double sided printing

The love of the LORD never fails.

Page left blank for double sided printing

May the LORD bless you!

_____

_____

_____

_____

_____

_____

_____

_____

_____

_____

He will cover you with his

feathers,

and under his wings you

will find refuge;

his faithfulness will be

your shield and rampart.

Page left blank for double sided printing

Page left blank for double sided printing

_____

_____

_____

_____

_____

_____

_____

_____

_____

_____

_____

_____

_____

_____

_____

_____

_____

_____

_____

_____

_____

_____

Page left blank for double sided printing

Page left blank for double sided printing

Page left blank for double sided printing

God's got the whole

world

in His hands

_____

_____

_____

_____

_____

_____

_____

_____

_____

_____

_____

Page left blank for double sided printing

Recipe:

TIME		SERVES		COOK TEMP
	INGREDIENTS			NOTES

DIRECTIONS

Recipe:

TIME		SERVES		COOK TEMP
	INGREDIENTS			NOTES

DIRECTIONS

Recipe:

TIME	SERVES	COOK TEMP

INGREDIENTS

NOTES

DIRECTIONS

Recipe:

TIME	SERVES	COOK TEMP

INGREDIENTS

NOTES

DIRECTIONS

Page left blank for double sided printing

Please cut these out to go with your rock Bible verse holder.

Matthew 6:33

But seek first his kingdom and his righteousness, and all these things will be given to you as well.

Romans 1:16

For I am not ashamed of the gospel, because it is the power of God that brings salvation to everyone who believes: first to the Jew, then to the Gentile.

The LORD is good to all; he has compassion on all he has made.

PSALM 145:8

Devote yourselves to prayer, being watchful & thankful.

COLOSSIANS 4:2

Proverbs 3:5

Trust in the Lord with all your heart and lean not on your own understanding.

Philippians 4:6

Do not be anxious about anything, but in every situation, by prayer and petition, with thanksgiving, present your requests to God.

PRONOUNS

- a word that is used to replace a noun in a sentence.

I	he	some
me	him	many
my	his	each
they	she	other
their	her	others
theirs	hers	what
them	this	who
we	that	whom
us	these	whose
our	those	
ours	all	
it	any	
its	both	

notes & OBSERVATIONS

Made in the USA
Coppell, TX
11 October 2024

38504355R00234